PSYCHODRAMA
for the Timid Clinician

Eva Leveton

Foreword by Virginia Satir

Illustrations by Arlene Goldbard

Springer Publishing Company
New York

No part of this publication may be reproduced, stored in a retrieval system, or transmitted, in any form or by any means, electronic, mechanical, photocopying, recording, or otherwise, without the prior permission of Springer Publishing Company, Inc.

Springer Publishing Company, Inc.
200 Park Avenue South
New York, N. Y. 10003

77 78 79 80 81 / 10 9 8 7 6 5 4 3 2 1

Illustrations by Arlene Goldbard, San Francisco

An earlier version of this work was published by the University of California, San Francisco, 1975.

Library of Congress Cataloging in Publication Data

Leveton, Eva.
   Psychodrama for the timid clinician.

   "An earlier version of this work was published by the University of California, San Francisco, 1975."
   Bibliography: p.
   1. Psychodrama.   I. Title. [DNLM:
1. Psychodrama.   2. Psychotherapy, Group.
WM430 L663p]
RC489.P7L49 1977   616.8'915   77–24574
ISBN 0-8261-2260-4
ISBN 0-8261-2261-2 pbk.

Printed in the United States of America

Contents

Foreword

This book is relevant, alive, and exceedingly helpful. It makes some of the seemingly very complicated parts of our human selves more understandable, and, therefore, more accessible to change. It is a treasure of resources, humor, techniques, earthy philosophy, together with practical ways to approach both old and new problems.

—Virginia Satir

Prologue

When I started my first psychodrama group I was not only timid but highly skeptical. I had ample reasons. I was untrained in the highly specialized techniques of Moreno's psychodrama and was, by my distrustful nature, inclined to label such techniques as "gimmicky." I wasn't sure if I could do it and, even if I *could*, I wasn't sure I wanted to—the story of my life. And, as in much of my life, it was typical for me to forge ahead, stumbling through many an awkward beginning, sustained by curiosity and the excitement of learning.

The time was the early '60s; the place, San Francisco—a place only beginning to feel the stirrings of those active iconoclasts which were to do much to revolutionize therapy. Family therapists were being trained at the Mental Research Institute in Palo Alto; Eric Berne's seminars attracted crowds of young people; we flocked to see a man named Fritz Perls demonstrate Gestalt techniques; we listened with a combination of timidity and excitement to such phrases as dance therapy, art therapy, body awareness—words wafting our way from the steamy hotsprings of Esalen. It was a time of experimentation, a time when many were learning and few qualified as experts.

When one of the larger day-treatment centers in San Francisco wanted to start a psychodrama group, it was difficult to find anyone to run it. A friend suggested that I try. She had known me long enough to know that, in addition to being a psychologist at U. C. Medical Center, I had been quite active in the theater—acting, directing, teaching. She also knew that I was interested in learning more about group therapy. I was interested—very interested—but scared. It occurred to me to read everything I could, fly to New York to Moreno's Institute, take a crash course; but I knew that I would not really profit from such extreme measures. I don't learn fast. And I have to start with what I know and can do in order to even begin to formulate the problems and questions with which I can use help from others. I decided that I would try it if it could be labeled an experiment, a learning experience for me. I wouldn't charge the center for the first six months, during which I would try to work out some techniques based on my own acting experience. The staff agreed.

I remember sitting on the stage of a large gymnasium facing about thirty people, most of whom looked forbiddingly tense, anxious, withdrawn. Usually, sitting on the stage with my legs dangling into the pit made me less nervous—I used to teach drama that way, leaping up to demonstrate if necessary. Not this time. I talked a little about the experimental nature of what we were doing. That helped. From now on at least I didn't have to be a "psychodramatist." And then I gave a beginning acting class. Simple sense memory exercises right out of Stanislavsky. One patient showed us in pantomime how she cleaned her room; another, how she prepared a meal. I saw that the act of performing these tasks was rewarding. People were proud of themselves for doing something. Patients were rewarded by therapists who felt equally intimidated by the notion of performance. We began to do pantomimes of arriving home after attending the center. Climbing the stairs, fumbling with the key, throwing down the coat, grabbing a drink, sitting down, a blank expression. Time after time either there was no one else living there or the meeting was an embarrassed, self-conscious one. When everyone had done something on the stage, we talked about how we felt. The empty, lonely feeling had been a shared experience. There were tears. People looked softer. I knew I would be continuing with psychodrama.

The center's staff helped me by leading the discussions following the work on stage. In this way I had a chance not only to learn something about group therapy, but also to evaluate the results of my techniques. Of course I began to read voraciously—Moreno, first and last. (I really think he's said everything there is to say in those phenomenal volumes, *Psychodrama, Volumes 1, 2*, and 3, Beacon, N.Y.: Beacon House, 1946; revised 1964. It only remains for the rest of us to focus on or illumine various aspects.) I also read pamphlets, chapters, anthologies, anything I could get. I attended some workshops given by the Morenos as well as by Moreno-trained individuals, including Dr. Richard Korn of Berkeley and Bobker ben Ali of Los Angeles. At the same time, I was caught up in the surge of active techniques involving encounter, art, and movement.

I have remained an eclectic. I found that my timidity rose to gigantic proportions whenever I expected myself to be a "something"—a psychodramatist, a facilitator of encounters, a movement or art therapist. I rebel against labels. I rebel against the use of another's vocabulary and that rebellion goes on inside me, while on the outside it is manifested by anxiety and tension. I found myself less timid when I made sure I wasn't promising something I couldn't deliver. I could promise that we would be using techniques related to drama and that we would work on problems involving the psyche; therefore, psychodrama still seemed the most appropriate name. I couldn't promise a "classical" Moreno-style approach and I do much to disabuse others, as I am disabusing you, dear reader, of that notion.

This book is an account of my experiments. For almost a decade I have continued to lead at least two weekly psychodrama groups in day centers or hospital wards, to give workshops in the use of my psychodramatic techniques, and to develop the use of these techniques as an adjunct to regular clinical practice with individuals, families, and groups. My aim is to let you know what techniques I've found useful, and to let you know as much as possible about my own experience in using the techniques: my hesitations, my questions, my conflicts. I would like this book to help give you the flavor of my process in leading psychodrama groups—to increase your choices in using similar techniques.

As I wrote this, I found myself more and more cramped by the voice of my conscience: *You can't do this, Eva. If you're going to call it psychodrama, you have to do it just as the Morenos teach it. You can't use just some of their knowledge, like taking what you like from a smorgasbord. And you can't just describe what you do. You have to theorize. You have to examine the theoretical background of Moreno's work. Compare it to Freud's. Feed in Lewinian field theory. Lead them through group therapy and clinch it with a fusion of Greek catharsis and the encounter group experience. They won't like you, Eva. They won't respect you.* If I could find a way to ignore these lectures I'd feel more at ease. Of course, I can't. I'm very timid about writing this book. Afraid of all the criticism. But I want to take the risk. My hope is that I can leave the theorizing to others for the time being. My wild dream is that Moreno will say, "It's alright, Eva. I'm delighted that you could use so many of my concepts, and that you acknowledge my work in developing them. Feel free to use only those techniques that fit your style and don't worry about the rest." Hopes and dreams don't always turn out—that's the risk.

Most of the techniques described in this book were originated by Moreno and some were begun by me. My goal is to provide the reader with an informal compendium of psychodramatic techniques and to describe in some detail my style in applying them.

Acknowledgments

I want to thank my husband, Alan Leveton, for helping me not only with his knowledgeable discussion but also by encouraging me to get this book out. I want to thank Virginia Satir, Bari Rolfe, and Judi Bryant for sharing their ideas with me and stimulating my own inventiveness. Howard Blatner helped me with his constructive criticism and his support. The staff of the Family Therapy Center in San Francisco helped me by reviewing each chapter as it was written. Florence Hagee and Suzanne Eldredge were particularly steadfast in giving me constructive criticism. Virginia Belport, our secretary, was tireless in her pursuit of my corrections and revisions. Thank you.

PSYCHODRAMA
for the Timid Clinician

Chapter 1

Who's in Charge?

Therapeutic disciplines offer many strategies for the therapist's control of his sessions with the patient. The timidity of many a therapist when faced with the use of the more active, experiential techniques has its roots in his early training, where he was imbued with messages like "be nondirective . . . don't initiate, facilitate . . . remain silent whenever possible . . . let the group members (or patient) make the major decisions about how the time is to be used." Our typical therapist—especially if his training occurred anytime before the mid-sixties, as mine did—is devilishly skilled in the art of subtle manipulation. He knows how to take charge of a session while acting the role of a blank screen upon which the patient is to project, or while listening with the third ear, or while sitting

1

silently, listening to a patient stretched out upon a couch. What he does not know is how to be clear and direct in taking charge of an activity: nothing in his training has prepared him for this eventuality. He feels he would seem blunt, insensitive, dictatorial, manipulative. He sits back timidly, afraid to take the risk.

At the present time there is a strong division among therapeutic orientations. The far left—activists all, spawned by Esalen and similar training grounds—is tired of talking and oriented toward finding activities which will teach lessons through experience rather than thought. The leader emerges as a strong figure in charge of coordinating the group's activities. The far right—their loyalty to Freud unshaken and confirmed by training institutes and analyses—maintains that insight alone produces change in the human psyche and that the only true methods for achieving it involve a strong one-to-one patient-therapist relationship which concerns itself largely with transference deduced exclusively from conversations about the patient's past and present circumstances. Here the leadership is subtle, nondirective in character. Most therapists are eclectics, carrying the division of both of these extremes inside them. I hope in the present chapter to discuss some ways of coping with the problem of direct leadership which avoid bluntness and insensitivity. Psychodrama—at least in its initial stages for any group—needs direct leadership.

Playground director, psychodrama director, theater director—all operate with the same paradox. Be spontaneous. Lead a play session. Direct the creative effort of the actor. Take charge of a group and teach them to become spontaneous and unafraid in role-playing important conflicts. Encourage spontaneity, but if someone tries to take over, let him know that he can't, lest the others be resentful. Encourage spontaneity, but if too many are spontaneously reticent, do something about it—this is an activity. Encourage spontaneity, but keep the group within some bounds and limits; this isn't the zoo.

Who will work today? Who will double? Who will play the various roles required in a given scene? What will we work on?

When I compare my behavior in a regular group therapy structure to my behavior in a psychodrama, I find myself taking a great deal more responsibility for the group's activities and for helping the group by finding the answers to the questions asked above. On the basis of whatever background information I can glean, I decide on the warm-up. Throughout the group, I am looking for those members of the group who seem eager to work, emotionally in touch with what is going on. They are the ones who will help me by making suggestions, volunteering services, taking part. They will help me but they are not in charge; I am.

The leader or director of a psychodrama must be able to model the "spontaneity" he wishes to elicit and to find ways of showing the group what can be done. He is facing people whose expectations vary greatly. Some think they have come to watch a spectacle. Others are afraid of being humiliated in a public display of their weaknesses. Many are interested in this potentially entertaining new form of learning something about themselves; very few have even the least idea of how to go about participating. Continuing with the paradox, the leader must find structures which will enable the group members to spontaneously express feelings in role playing. The process of deciding what structures to use involves a great deal of sensitivity to group behavior—unless, of course, one has a taste for the purely dictatorial approach.

When my psychodrama groups are part of the program of an ongoing institution—psychiatric ward, probation department, school—I usually make it a point to talk to someone in touch with the members of my group before I meet them. My "contact" may be able to tell me much that will help me in choosing the type of warm-up to use and the type of work the group is ready for. I try to find out something about the group atmosphere—whether it's depressed and gloomy, rebellious, efficient, hardworking. Another aspect which always interests me is any problem which may have concerned the group as a whole: a staff-patient conflict; the departure of an important member; conflicts about house or institute rules. My informant often provides me with valuable information about individual group members. He describes who has been the center of attention or the butt of the others' resentment, who seems interested and ready to work, who is just sitting and observing. Armed with such information, I am already a few steps away from arbitrary decisions.

From the moment I first encounter the members of my group—with or without prebriefing—I gather further information which helps me plan. I make it a practice to spend a few minutes in informal chatter with group members. This enables me to make a warm, informal contact and also to assess the group atmosphere, which members seem shy, which members seem to be interested and eager to know me, what relationships exist in the group.

Information about the group I am to lead also helps me develop realistic expectations of our work. A slow, quiet group can be termed successful if most of its members participate even with only a slight show of feeling. A more lively group can be expected to role-play more actively. The more realistic I can be in my expectations, the freer I will be to "hang loose," to encourage and validate the group's productions, rather than to pull and tug in a direction which the group members can't or won't reach.

My warm-up has a great deal to do with what I have learned thus far. If the group is reputed to be shy, somewhat depressed, and resistant to working, I may start with the simplest of warm-ups (asking each member to think of a question he could ask someone else in the group; asking each member to say a sentence he has enjoyed hearing from another member of this family, for example). My goal here is building confidence by giving everyone a chance to participate successfully. I will be very careful, in building on this warm-up, that I do not ask anyone to work further unless he is ready. Any rejections I collect will add to the listlessness of the already depressed group. I may continue to work with the whole group for several rounds until I see someone intent on pursuing something further, at which point, again, it will be up to me to find a form for his work.

I may work quite differently with a group whose members have shown strength and interest in working on their problems, and who receive me with some vitality and curiosity. My choice for a warm-up will be a dramatic one (to portray, in a few sentences, the most difficult character in your life; to portray an authority figure such as a staff member, teacher, or doctor evaluating you). I may interrupt the warm-up in order to begin to work with an individual and then continue with the warm-up's task. In this kind of a group I don't have to worry so much about exclusion, rejection, and depression. I can work with one individual for a while, continue with the warm-up, and work with another.

I have done some experimenting with the role of leader, trying a more nondirective approach, hoping that leadership would emerge from the group and that I might sit back and contribute my services by playing a role or doubling. These experiments have convinced me that a psychodrama group is vastly more productive with strong leadership than when left to its own devices. The leaderless group—or the group that uses a leader only as consultant—spends a great deal of time overcoming initial resistances, negotiating about what is to be done and how to do it. I can imagine instances in which this might be considered time well spent. If, for example, the group is a training group which will be getting together for a set time period to learn about group dynamics and psychodrama, this kind of slow-motion look at resistances could prove educational. In most of my work, however, I prefer to use my energy providing strong leadership for structuring psychodramatic work rather than sitting back watching the group struggle with its own resistances until a manner of working emerges.

The strong leader helps encourage spontaneity by providing the security of an authority figure. The role may resemble that of parent or teacher of young children in allowing group members to feel: *I can play, I can try whatever silly thing I want to because there's the leader keeping an eye on us; the leader won't let the others hurt me and she'll stop me from hurting others; I can try whatever I think is right, the leader will tell me if it isn't.*

The strong leader helps members contribute feelings and personal conflicts by being responsible for structuring the work. The group member feels: *I can bring up my problem and the leader will figure out a way to work on it. I have something I want to talk about but I don't know what I want to do with it, I don't know if I should ask the others to play roles in my family, I don't want to ask someone to double for me.*

The strong leader gives permission for a great many things that group members would like to do but inhibit because of shyness and reticence. The leader helps the group member to pick the others who are to participate in his scene. He also asks the member to portray his feelings as dramatically as possible, to yell if he wants to, to put his tender feelings into words, to continue and prolong a given scene—in each instance giving permission, validating the group member in a task that would be more difficult if he were to make all these decisions himself.

The greatest problem, of course, that the strong leader faces is that of remaining sensitive to the group so that he is not an unfeeling, inappropriate dictator. My own decisions are based on information about the group: my informant's discussion, my own perceptions. If the group's reaction makes me question this information, it is extremely important to get more response from group members before proceeding. I may have suggested the wrong warm-up. If the group's responses are halting, listless, boring, I may double for a group member, saying "What is this she's asking us to do? I don't want to do it. It's like nursery school. It's boring." If I get some response, I will change the warm-up. The other group members may want to say something about the warm-up, and the responses will clue me in to a more appropriate theme.

There are times when a particular scene has affected the group strongly and in such a way that it is hard for the group members to continue with the scene. Difficult themes such as suicide, murderous feelings, or drug addiction often produce a group reaction of silence, distractedness, disconnectedness. In this situation, I want to hear what the group members are feeling before deciding what to do next. I may say, "It looks like everybody felt pretty strongly about what just went on. Could we each finish the sentence 'What really touched me was . . .'?" The answers will give me a chance to find out about similar situations in the group members' own lives, which will provide material for further scenes.

There are times when I, the leader, can't make up my mind about a warm-up or scene because I have several options open to me. I will ask the group, "We could start by saying a sentence about this group, or by doing something nonverbal, or by working on family themes. Which appeals to you, John?" I have found that my questions are answered immediately if I address them to specific members rather than to the group in general. Asking two or three individuals and taking account of the other group members' nonverbal responses help me decide on the task.

As leader, I must remain sensitive to my own feelings as well as to those of the group. I have to tune in to myself and to others for information about the group's togetherness in any given endeavor. When I sense discomfort in myself it may be important to tell the group what it is and ask if anyone else feels it. When I sense discomfort in the group, it is important to check this out with group members.

This constant checking of the group's reactions as well as my own provides the most reliable safeguard I know against insensitivity and arbitrary rule. I find it helpful to have eye contact with as many of the group members as I can during any one session. I pay attention to any movement or noise in the group; these clues may provide valuable information about a member's emotional involvement in a given scene. (They may, of course, only provide information about the hardness of the chairs—but it's worth checking.) The eye messages I exchange during a given scene with group members who are in the audience add to the group cohesiveness. A group member sees that his leader cares about his reaction, that not only those in the scene have the leader's attention. During a scene I may make nonverbal comments on audience members' sadness, anxiety or tension, usually by quickly mirroring the physical position or facial expression. After the scene, I often check these impressions out. For example, I may say, "John, you seemed really tense during the last scene. Did you feel tense? Did the scene have some relevance for you?"

During the years of my own greater timidity, when I was first beginning to lead groups, I felt greatly pressured to "get the show on the road" and regarded the kind of discussion just described as a possible impediment to the dramatic situations I wanted to create. The longer I've worked, the more I find that a slower rhythm is vastly more productive. It's true, there is no blare of trumpets followed by a dimming of the houselights in preparation for a drama which unfolds before the undividedly attentive audience. What happens usually starts with a quiet conversation which grows in intensity and may even unfold into an intense drama. But the drama can be interrupted to clarify misunderstandings or to change the focus to an audience member who has burst into tears. We move by fits and starts. Whatever the rhythm, the leader's activity is decisive in determining the psychodrama's course.

Chapter 2

Seating Arrangements

Moreno describes a mouth-wateringly appealing setup in which to do psychodrama: a gently sloping semicircular seating arrangement for the audience, a series of wide platforms which bridge the space between audience and stage, a stage equipped with light and sound effects which facilitate the recreation of a great variety of settings. Needless to say, I have yet to run into either a hospital or therapy center—not to mention clubs or schools—where even an approximation of such a setting exists. The usual accommodations vary. There may be a middle-sized room with rows of chairs and a desk at the front, the classroom; a room with chairs arranged in a circle, the group therapy room; a room with desks and chairs arranged in a "U" or "banquet" shape, the conference room; or a

9

vast auditorium with a small, badly-lit wooden stage and rows
of ancient chairs arranged in front of it. The latter may show
signs of having been used as a gymnasium at one time. Usually
it is half-empty and creates a thunderous theatrical entrance
for any member of the group who appears late.

The ideal setting rarely appears in reality and, though
eminently desirable, is not necessary. The basis of psychodrama is improvisation, make-believe. Any space can be
turned into your living room, the boss's office, a courtroom, a
garden. Any space can become a stage. I react negatively to
most of the rooms I've entered with the intention of doing
psychodrama. It's partly that I'm a somewhat rebellious, cantankerous individual extremely sensitive to structures and
rules. Oh, a conference room—this is a place where you're
supposed to talk, brainstorm, to SIT. No way to see anyone's
body. The regularity of the circle in the group therapy room
spells uniformity, evenness. No room for chaos. No expectation
that there might be "a scene."

My rebelliousness led me to search for something new. I
started by asking people to rearrange the room in some way
that would be comfortable for them and to leave some room
for a stage area. I soon learned that this was an excellent
warm-up activity; in fact, I was communicating something of
great relevance to the promotion of further work. The message
goes something like this: *I'm your leader and if I feel irritated
by the way this room looks, I admit it. We don't have to accept
things the way they are. In this group we can change things.
There's some room for chaos here. It's not a free-for-all, I'm
still in charge, and I'm mainly asking you to seat yourself
where and as you want to. But this is a structure where we can
play around, have some fun, make some noise.*

Most rooms carry a message: 'Be smart.' 'Be sensitive.'
'Relax.' 'Watch the show.' The message will often add to the
group inhibitions unless it is labeled or counteracted in some
way.

By now you will have guessed my first requirement in seating arrangements: flexibility. A bare room with pillows or
light and easily movable chairs is preferable. Most of the time,

people in my groups sit in a circle using the middle as the stage area. I encourage informality. I move around a good deal myself and am glad to see others do so. If some people want to sit on the floor, I usually join them. I discourage "hiding" (sitting directly behind someone else, watching from the doorway); however, if I discover that any closer commitment produces fear in a person, I prefer his coming and "hiding" to his not coming at all.

My own movement in the group usually proceeds as follows. I start by sitting somewhere in the circle and I tell the group something about myself. Whether the group is new to me or not, I know that they're watching me keenly and I believe that some information about my feelings will help them make more sense out of my behavior. Then I start the warm-up. From here on in, I try to remain flexible so that I can sit next to the individual who is working on something which seems important, which could be developed a little further. In the following example, the warm-up task was to express irritation with someone in the family.

Emily says, "I'm talking to my mom: 'Mom, stop treating me like a baby. I'm 21 years old. It really makes me mad when you do that.'"

I get up from my chair and sit next to Emily, asking the person next to her to change seats with me. "I'm your mother, Emily, and I can't help worrying about you. You just don't show any responsibility," I say.

Emily proceeds to argue with me (her mother) for a bit. When she says, "We do this over and over again and it's always the same," I drop out of my role and ask her if she is willing to come back to this problem and work some more on it after the warm-up. When we do, group members are already familiar with the basic conflict, and role-playing and doubling is less difficult. As a scene is set up in the middle of the room, or in any "stage area," there is usually reluctance on the part of the main character or protagonist (in this case, Emily) to step into the limelight. Again, I try to help bridge this transition by moving into the center with Emily. I ask her to describe the living room where she talks with Mom. As she sets the stage, I usually sit or kneel next to her so that the other group members aren't blocked from seeing by my position. As she begins talking with her mother, I move back to the periphery again and usually remain standing somewhere in the circle so that I can move around, asking others to participate in the scene or participating myself when I want to.

It is very important to me that the stage itself be a flexible area. Even in rooms equipped with a regular stage, I may want to move to a circular or semicircular arrangement of the group either on stage or in the auditorium. The room itself may provide various areas, each appropriate for a particular scene setting. During one psychodrama session, a different area may be used to suit each different scene. A family drama can be set in the part of the room where a sofa and some upholstered chairs are located; a later scene may make use of the large space in the middle of the room in order to depict the social room of the hospital with group members moving on and off stage as they spontaneously take roles in the scene; the last scene of the day may take place in yet a different area of the room where a desk is located, suitable for use in a job interview drama.

Working with very distressed patients in hospital wards often means working with individuals who have talked very little for weeks, who move rigidly and slowly, who seldom look at the others in the room. To ask this kind of person to step up on the stage, speak loudly enough to be heard, and show us what ails him is asking him for more than he is willing to give. His dramatic statement is his withdrawal. At the same time, he may want to come out of his quietness and tell us something about himself if we don't make it too hard. I may start my work with him by sitting next to him and talking quietly. If I get any sense that he wants to work further, I may ask some of the other group members to come and sit near him, taking roles relevant to his dilemma. This strategy often helps the reticent patient work, but may lead to frustration for other group members who are sitting too far away for easy hearing. If this is the case, I again encourage the group members to move closer to the stage area. I explain to the group that it's hard for John to talk much louder at this time, and that it would be more expedient for the other group members to come closer in order to facilitate better hearing. The lessened formality and greater physical closeness of the group members often act as further emotional support for the protagonist.

Groups are not always filled with reticent patients. On the contrary, psychodrama groups are often attended by individuals whose energy and sense of excitement increases with the thought of being "on stage." Adolescents filled with the drama of their conflicts with unsympathetic authority figures often fit this category. People with some penchant for acting or some actual acting experience may associate the stage with an opportunity to show emotion, to get in touch with fantasies, to try on other roles. If a stage is available, I may use it in working with these individuals; they often infect others with their enthusiasm. Afterwards, I may shift back to "the round" to work with less stagestruck group members.

Flexibility is all. If group members can sit where they like, move when they need to, spontaneity is increased. If the stage can be anywhere, the imagination is challenged and stage fright, often a reaction to the kind of dramatic focus of attention inherent in a real stage, can be relegated to a place of lesser importance.

Chapter 3

The Warm-Up

As a family therapist accustomed to the intense, immediate focus characteristic of a family in crisis, the idea of a warm-up was difficult for me to accept when I started my work with groups. Who needed a warm-up? Pain is strong and each one of us lives out a multitude of psychodramas. There wasn't any need to waste time in some kind of "artificial group activity." I thought: the thing to do is to plunge in. Go in with the expectation that group members want to work on their problems, ask for volunteers, and find a dramatic form which will help produce insight, catharsis, and several alternative solutions.

By now, the reader will have guessed that the above account depicts a therapeutic optimism bound to run up against resistance, a theme to be discussed in detail later on. Each venture in personal growth is bound by paradox. *I want to change but*

I don't want to risk anything new. I want to risk something new but I'm afraid I might change. Anything's better than what's happening now. Anything's better than the unknown. A psychodrama group carries some additional resistances peculiar to any event described by the words acting, role-playing, psychodrama, staging. *Do you have to be able to act? I'm not an actor. I can't be phony, pretend to be someone else. Do you have to perform? In front of an audience? They'll just make a fool of me, make me act out my problems and then ridicule me. Who is that new lady? A patient? Oh, she leads it. What's she going to make us do? I heard they really got emotional here last week—Anne left crying that day. I don't want that to happen to me. Not in front of the whole group. I'm just going to sit quietly and hope she doesn't look at me.*

Slowly, I learned that both the group members and I needed a warm-up, a relatively neutral activity in which all who wanted to could participate, which would give us a chance to get to know each other a little. By "relatively neutral" I mean that the warm-up should be a task which affords the participant a good deal of choice regarding the amount of personal disclosure he is willing to make. In addition, of course, the warm-up should carry a message about the nature of the group work, that it is dramatic, experiential in quality, as opposed to other therapies which might be classified as more introspective and analytic. In my psychodrama groups, I discourage "talking about" an event whenever I can, or at least I keep it to a minimum, preferring the participant to show us by doing wherever possible: rather than talking about his father, portraying him; rather than describing a crisis that took place at home, finding some people in the group who could play the important roles, clueing them in, and acting out the basic conflicts.

The following are some examples of verbal and nonverbal group warm-ups. These tasks will provide the leader with valuable information about the group members' willingness or eagerness to participate, give him clues about whether there are any problem areas common to several members of the group (always a preferable choice for later, more detailed work), inform him as to which group members react strongly to each other. By setting up a warm, easygoing atmosphere, the warm-up also gives the leader an opportunity to dispel some of the misconceptions about a psychodrama group by rewarding responses and encouraging and supporting shyer members. The best kind of warm-up has some relationship to other group activities. In groups which have a common bond, these are easily thought up.

A group of teachers, for example, can easily be paired off and asked to think of a specific teacher-pupil conflict. I may begin by asking the group to form pairs. The next task is a simple one. Each member of a pair has to choose to be either No. 1 or No. 2. When everyone has made his choice I ask the 1's to be teachers, the 2's to be pupils, and request that each pair decide on a specific teacher-pupil conflict which they would like to act out. As each pair works—the task can be done sitting around a circle if the group is shy, or the pairs can be asked to work in the center of the room, or on a stage, if there is one—we will gain enough information to run several sessions.

On a psychiatric ward, a community meeting with compulsory attendance precedes my weekly session. Often, the nurse's description of what went on in the meeting will provide a warm-up. The content of one meeting concerned planning the day-patients' activities on weekends. A lot of apparent helplessness and loneliness had appeared to be beneath the surface, but the patients' discussion had circumvented the painful emotions by centering on plans for weekend picnics, bus rides to the park, etc. The warm-up consisted of asking each patient to imagine himself coming home from the hospital that Friday night and to show us what happens, using some chairs and existing doors for scenery and speaking his thoughts out loud. Needless to say, the warm-up became more and more poignant and the feelings of isolation and helplessness did not remain below the surface.

Often, however, little or no information about the group's background or recent experience is available. No warm-up suggests itself, and, as I look around the circle of expectant faces, I feel less and less sure of what I want to do. I need a warm-up which will both acquaint me with the group and provide us with a common experience. At such times, I choose techniques gleaned from encounter groups, acting classes, party games, body movement work—in short, from wherever I can find them. Some examples follow.

Verbal Warm-Ups

1. *Directions:* "I have a ball. While it's in my hands I can talk. Without it I can't. Whoever catches the ball— whoever has it in his hands—has to talk. The others can't." The next step involves an important decision for the leader. What will he say before he tosses the ball to someone else? Solutions range from "Who are you? Tell me something about yourself," to more structured tasks such as "I'm your mother, what have you got to say to me?" or "If you were an animal (an actor, a character in a fairy tale or television show, a plant, etc.), what would you be?" When I have asked my question, I toss the ball to the person whose response I want, telling him to throw it to someone else when he has answered me. If two people get into a prolonged discussion, throwing the ball back and forth between them, I may try to catch the ball in order to ask that each person try to include someone new when he asks his question or makes his challenge, so that the warm-up reaches as many members of the group as possible.
   Discussion: This is an excellent warm-up for a large group in a large room such as a gym or auditorium, in which the ball can be rolled or tossed freely. A small space inhibits spontaneity because the ball can't be thrown freely.
2. *Directions:* "Look around the room in silence for a few minutes. Find someone whom you don't know very well and ask that person a question."
   Discussion: This is an unthreatening warm-up, easily performed by a somewhat timid group. In leading this warm-

up, it is important to accept questions and answers which may appear undramatic and somewhat superficial at first. The first task is to provide a context in which the ice can be broken. Once this is done and there is a flow of questions and answers, the task can be intensified emotionally by the leader's saying, "That's good. Now I'd like you to try a slightly different type of question. From now on, I'd like you to ask questions relating to feelings." If the task means asking questions of relative strangers, I may add, "As you looked at the person you chose, you probably had some idea of how he felt. Maybe you could tell him what you thought and check it out with him." If the task involves questioning a person who elicits strong feelings, I may say, "You have strong feelings about the person you want to question. Maybe you could tell him something about them and find out something about his response." As people work, the leader has a chance to ask questions of his own pertaining to feelings which the group members may have about the other person, his family members, friends, or job situation. With this information, it is easy to plan work for the rest of the group's time.

3. *Directions:* "Think of a sentence you'd really like to hear (wouldn't want to hear) from someone else in this room, or from a friend or member of your family. Be that person and say the sentence."

Discussion: This task, especially in the first, positive version, is the most supportive warm-up I know of. I frequently use it on the psychiatric hospital ward when the atmosphere is one of passive depression. Patients who have been unable to participate in other group work often respond to this task. It has the surprising advantage of providing a quick pathway to some intense emotional experiences which can be used for further work. One woman responded by saying, for example, "I'm my own son, and he's saying, 'I still care for you even if I don't write.'" It was easy to set up a scene in which she confronted him with her feelings about him.

In the negative version, this warm-up gives people a chance to air complaints in a satirical way. The task often engenders a good deal of laughter and fellow feeling as some of the remarks we all dread hearing are aired. "I'm my wife: 'You're late again, Jim.'". . . . "I'm my son: 'Dad, why can't I have the car tonight?'" . . . "I'm my mother: 'I've waited up for you all night.'" . . . "I'm my boss: 'You're fired.'" Again, this is a task which provides a natural transition for further work.

4. *Directions:* "Pretend that this social club (school, office, psychiatric ward, therapy center) is a person standing in the middle of the room. Talk to him. Complain, demand, plead, etc. Maybe you want to thank him for something. You can do this also."

   Discussion: This is a warm-up which provides a lot of valuable information about a group's common experience to a leader who is new to the group. Also, when I have information suggesting some conflicts in the group, this warm-up can provide a forum for airing them. For example, our social club may be having difficulty getting members to do the work necessary to support its functioning, an office may have endured recent clashes between its liberal and conservative elements, a psychiatric ward may have sent some valuable group member to another hospital, etc. If these conflicts are in the air, this warm-up provides a forum for talking about them and using them for further work.

5. *Directions:* "Be someone in your family (someone important to you) describing you in a sentence or two." This task has many variations, e.g.: "Choose another person in this group. Be that person talking about you"; "Be your therapist (teacher, group leader, boss) and tell us about the progress you are making."

   It is important to demonstrate this task as soon as possible after giving the directions, as it is difficult to describe and may elicit some confusion which can be avoided by an example. Rather than answering questions, I usually say something like, "Let me show you what I mean. I'm

Charles over there and I'm thinking: 'What is Eva up to now? I hope this isn't as hard as it sounds. I don't even get it.'"

Discussion: This warm-up gives the group an immediate participating acquaintance with role reversal and provides a great deal of information as well as easy, natural transitions to further scenes. People who are somewhat verbal and outgoing often enjoy portraying someone important, especially if they know in advance that the portrayal does not have to be long and detailed.

6. *Directions:* "Think of your favorite game or pastime when you were a child. Think of yourself playing the game, think of what you looked like, sounded like, what your surroundings were—until you can really see and feel yourself as you were then." A 3-to-5-minute silence follows. "Now, staying at the age level you've just thought about, tell us your name—you may have a nickname, I don't know—how old you are, and what your favorite game is."

Discussion: This warm-up facilitates the awakening of vivid childhood memories. In conducting it, it is important to insist that the participants make their contributions *as* the child that experienced the game, rather than talking *about* the experience as an adult recalling his childhood. The role-playing will help recall other childhood experiences useful for further work. This particular warm-up facilitates work in the area of social experience—the joy of being accepted, 'having a friend,' the dreaded rejections by other children, by the coach, the teacher, the scout leader.

Another warm-up that recalls vivid childhood memories, in ways more idiosyncratic for each individual, follows.

7. *Directions:* "Think of yourself as a child. Choose whatever age first vividly suggests itself to you. Give yourself some little time to really place yourself at that age, so that you can reexperience what it was like to be you then. You may close your eyes if you wish." A 3-to-5-minute silence

follows. "Now, I'd like you to remain in the role you've just been thinking about and tell us how a typical day passes for you. Start by telling us when and where exactly you wake up and go on from there."

Discussion: All warm-ups involving childhood memories provide astoundingly vivid recall, which is often surprising to the participant, who hadn't realized how exactly he had stored his early experiences. This phenomenon has several consequences for the leader. He must understand that participants may need more support and encouragement in this warm-up than with other tasks—they are often genuinely out of touch with their usual adult defenses and feel unusually vulnerable. Most of the time the memories produced are recalled with a mixture of feelings—some anxiety, some remembered warmth—and the participants have a delightful and real sense of rediscovery.

There are also times when an individual recalls an important childhood experience so vividly that he may appear to be "stuck" there and the leader may need to help him make a bridge back to his present adult role. This can be accomplished in several ways, one of the most efficient of which seems to me to be to ask the individual to make some "then-and-now" statements. ("Then I felt little, now I don't feel little but I still feel insecure; then I was never mad, now I get irritated easily.") Other methods are: (1) to give the individual a second exercise which duplicates the warm-up except that he is to use the silent time to think himself back to his present self and environment; (2) to ask the individual to see if he can form a mental image of himself as a child and then another of himself as a man and to describe what he sees; (3) to ask the individual to recall his present self and then to have a conversation with the child-self he just role-played by using an empty chair. (See chapter on Gestalt techniques entitled "The Empty Chair.")

There is yet one other childhood recall technique which I use quite frequently: writing with the unaccustomed hand. This will be described in the nonverbal warm-ups section of this chapter.

8. *Directions:* "I'm going to give you a sentence and I want you to fill in the blanks. The sentence is, 'In this group I'm a . . . (I feel . . ., I want . . ., I can . . .); outside of this group I'm a . . . (I feel . . ., I want . . ., I can . . .).' It doesn't matter how you fill in the blanks. I'll start by saying, 'In this group I'm a psychodrama leader; outside I'm a gardener who is having a hard time with the deer who eat my beans.'"

   Discussion: This is another technique which helps break the ice in a shy group where many people need a great deal of structure to participate. It is unthreatening, can start off superficially and be intensified with several go-rounds, and provides a great deal of information helpful for further work. Its disadvantage is that it is not dramatic and that there will have to be a transition before the role-playing begins. This is usually easily accomplished by exploring some of the material brought to light during the warm-up and dramatizing it.

9. *Directions:* "I'm going to give you a sentence to finish. The sentence is 'The next step I want to take in my life is. . . .'"

   Discussion: I have used this warm-up quite successfully when someone in the group has just taken a new step in his life which has come up in informal conversation before the group starts. I may, for example, hear that Henrietta, who has just graduated from high school, has successfully applied for her first job. As the group starts, I will call this fact to the group's attention, discuss it in a little more detail with Henrietta in front of the group, and then proceed with the warm-up.

   This exercise is also a rather static, undramatic warm-up, but one which provides a relatively safe beginning as well as a good deal of information for further work. The leader might then ask each group member something about what would be involved in his taking his next step, what would favor his doing so, what would hinder him, and use the answers to set up further scenes.

10. *Directions:* "Today I want you to try something really different. I want you to fantasize a dream existence. If you weren't who you are, who would you like to be? Where would you live, what would you do with yourself? You can choose any life-style you've ever heard about."

Discussion: In a group where some spontaneity and willingness to deal with fantasy exists, this warm-up can be quite exciting. The Walter Mitty in each of us takes great pleasure in being given an airing. Group members often develop a delightful sense of spontaneous play in this warm-up which can be extended by scenes in which the individual chooses others in the group to help him role-play in creating his fantasy existence. In one of our groups, for example, a famous ship captain conducted interviews with other group members applying for jobs on his ship during its impending world tour; in another a millionaire chose to assign roles to two women who portrayed world-renowned *femmes fatales* fighting over him.

I expect each member of the group to participate in the warm-up whenever possible. In a group too large to permit this, I try to structure a warm-up which can be answered in one sentence or one word, in order to permit as many people to participate as possible. The psychodrama group leader must find strategies which will help him insure maximum participation. Some of mine follow.

I try to achieve a middle ground between utter spontaneity—which could result in one member's dominating the group and many others excluding themselves from the warm-up—and rigid leader control, which can have the effect of reducing spontaneity, creating the feeling among group members that they must look to the leader for every move. Thus, in relatively spontaneous groups, I tend to sit back and wait for individuals to respond as they feel ready. When the time-lag between participants increases, or when I see the group participation coming to a close before all of the members have participated, I encourage those who haven't spoken to do so. In groups whose spontaneity is low, I often ask a staff member (or anyone whom I know I can trust to cooperate) to begin, and then I proceed around the circle, asking each person to participate. If an individual is reluctant to participate, I usually give some support and encouragement by further structuring the task for him (see the chapter on resistances) and then asking him to try it again. In case of an out-and-out refusal, I usually ask the individual to listen to some of the other responses, telling him that I will come back to him at the end to see if he's changed his mind.

One of the warm-up's primary functions is to create an atmosphere of spontaneity and trust in a very short time period. The tasks themselves present the group with a common bond. The leader has to see to it that the process of warming up takes place, that the tasks are not mechanically performed. It is crucial to encourage or praise any contribution. The warm-up should provide a supportive atmosphere in which the individual can take his first steps in sharing personal information; therefore, it is helpful to thank each participant by a nod, smile, a short comment about his contribution, or a literal "thank you." A warm-up functions at its optimum if it gains momentum as it proceeds—group members join in more and more rapidly, respond to each other, relaxing their defensive formality or stiffness. Group members expect to fail. *I don't know what she wants us to do. I'm not at all sure I understand what she said. Well, I'll try—but I probably won't get it right.* If the group leader validates this sense of impending doom by apparently judging a response as mistaken, not enough, too sparse, or not quite right, the group's spirit immediately sags and the momentum cannot build.

In the event that a group member actually misunderstands the task, the group leader confronts a small dilemma. He thinks: *I'd like to validate this response but how can I when it's wrong? The others will now become confused about what they're supposed to do. On the other hand, correcting this fellow in front of all these people isn't easy.* The group members, many of whom are aware of the misunderstanding, think: *Well, here it is. Just what I thought would happen to me. He made a fool of himself. What if she tells him? How humiliating. What if she doesn't? That wouldn't be right either.* My own strategy in this dilemma involves two steps. First I validate his contribution. For example, let's say the warm-up involves speaking some sentences John's therapist would say about him. John, however, says some sentences to his therapist. My first response is, "Thanks. Sounds like you have some pretty strong feelings about that guy." Then, having stuck to my dictum: "Never let a response go by without validation," I go on to the second step, which involves clarifying the warm-up for John. "Could you try one other thing? Play the role of your therapist, Dr. Rosen, and tell us about John. O.K.?" In order to be as clear as possible I may then repeat the direction to the next person. "Let's hear your therapist talking about you." With this strategy, I can often avoid the bogging down of the group which results from either ignoring the mistaken response or from downgrading it.

Another dilemma presents itself to the leader who has chosen the wrong warm-up. As he watches the process, he notices wooden responses, a lack of enthusiasm—no momentum at all. The process seems more reminiscent of a freeze-out. In that case, I change the warm-up. If I have any clue in the form of a small spark that momentarily flickered somewhere and then fizzled, I use it for my next attempt. If not, I may try something nonverbal, if the first warm-up was verbal, or anything that takes us in a radically different direction. Before making the change, I check out my perception with the group. "Would you rather stick with this warm-up or try something else?" This gives me a chance to check on my own paranoia (there are times when the fizzle is inside me and the group chooses to continue with the task) and enables group members to be part of the decision to change. Any willingness to change on the part of the leader has an additional advantage: it models an aspect of spontaneity. It conveys the message: *In this group you don't have to stick to anything rigidly. You can change to something more fun when you feel bogged down.*

Nonverbal warm-ups have the obvious advantage of requiring no talk at all—a considerable advantage when encountering a group of strangers, a group reluctant to open up. Of course there are resistances here also: *This is silly. Like nursery school. Is it going to be one of those things where they make you touch each other? I don't want to touch anybody in this group! I don't want to pantomime anything. That's like charades!* The nonverbal group warm-up provides the group with an ongoing process which can be shared and reworked in psychodramatic terms. These tasks get group members out of their chairs, already an activity quite different from regular therapy. Nonverbal warm-ups have one disadvantage: they require an extra transitional step before actual role-playing can start. Most of these tasks need to be followed by some group discussion during which the leader gets clues for further work from the answers to questions like: "What was that like for you? Do you have anything you want to say to any other member of the group? To me? Have you felt similarly in any other life situation?"

Nonverbal Warm-Ups

1. Rearranging the room. (This applies especially where the room has been set up in a formal way—rows of chairs, chairs around tables, etc.)
   Directions: "I would like to begin by changing the room around. We need some space for a stage. And I want you to be comfortable. So make some decisions about how and where you want to sit—chairs, floor, table, next to whom—and where the stage could be. I would like you to accomplish this task silently. If you need to communicate with someone, do it in pantomime." (Take 5–10 minutes.)
   Discussion: This warm-up usually creates an atmosphere of play—it is reminiscent of the child's setting up his play room. It is somewhat more successful in larger groups of over 20 people, as choice increases with the size of the group. One caution: if the group members appear as stiff as the furnishings of the room, do not use this warm-up. It has meaning only when the task is welcomed at least by some of the group members. I usually follow this task with

yet another warm-up—the verbal childhood memory exercises described earlier seem particularly apt.

2. Walking. (This task is possible only in a room large enough to permit some freedom of movement.) Both this technique and "stamping" come from movement therapy.

Directions: "I would like to start by moving around a little. So, I'd like you first of all to get out of your chairs. (*It is always important to get the group to its feet as soon as possible—otherwise they will sit and listen.*) Get in touch with the space around you. Don't talk. Take a look at where you're standing, who's standing near you, who's far away. (*Allow about 2 minutes.*) Now start to walk slowly around the room taking in everything and everyone with your eyes. Don't talk and don't touch anyone if you can help it. (*Allow 2–5 minutes.*) Now increase your speed and avoid eye contact. Walk faster. Change your pattern if you have one. Faster. (*Allow 2–3 minutes.*) If you are about to bump into someone, don't stop yourself—unless you have some private objection. Let yourself be jostled. Avoid eye contact. (*Allow 2 minutes.*) Stop. Tune in to yourself for a minute to get in touch with your feelings. Notice any body sensations. (*Allow 1 minute.*) Now walk slowly again, making eye contact, and let yourself make some physical contact if you want to. (*Allow 2–5 minutes.*) Good. Let's stop now and come back to the circle." This exercise can also be ended by saying, as the last part ends, "I would now like you to find a partner (form groups of 3, 5, etc.)—still without talking—and stop when you've done so." At the end of a few minutes, check to see whether anyone is without a partner and help him find one. In groups where members do not know one another, this is an easy way to choose partners for further work.

Discussion: I've often used this warm-up with day-long workshops which start in the morning. It is a good wake-up as well as warm-up exercise. It is easily performed even by inhibited groups—it has the advantage of being easy to do and yielding a lot of group contact and active movement.

The discussion afterwards most often centers around the experience of making eye contact, an experience which calls up many associated feelings about trust, intimacy, shyness, and privacy and provides a natural bridge to further work.

3. Writing with the unaccustomed hand, a movement therapy technique. Some materials are necessary: paper, preferably large pieces which can be torn off a roll of butcher paper or from a large sketch pad, and crayons, charcoal, or pencils.

   Directions: "Today I'd like to try something which most of you probably haven't tried before: Writing with your unaccustomed hand. If you're right-handed, that means your left—otherwise vice versa. Writing this way often helps you say something you feel and remember things you've forgotten. In order to get into it, I'd like you to give yourselves a fantasy of yourself when you were first learning to write. Where were you—at home, school, nursery school? Picture the details of your environment. Picture yourself as you were then. How old were you? What did it feel like to be you then? You can close your eyes if you wish." I give these directions in a soft, rather unobtrusive voice so that I don't interfere with the group's focus of concentration. Then I wait about five minutes, encouraging group members to stay with their fantasy and discouraging any talk. "When you feel ready, I'd like you to pick up a crayon and tear off a piece of paper to write on. Stay with your fantasy of yourself. Find a place to write—the floor, your chair, the table over there. Now, I'd like you to practice writing your name. If you had a nickname, maybe you could practice writing that."

   At this point, I usually begin to take on a shade of the first-grade teacher, further encouraging the group in focusing on an earlier time in their lives. After about five minutes, I continue: "Now, still with your unaccustomed hand, I'd like you to try writing a little story about yourself as you are in your fantasy of first learning to write. Tell us your name, how old you are, and anything else you want us to know. See if you can just let your hand do the writing, write what it tells you, try not to think it out." After people start to write, I notice the ones who are finished and discourage their comparing notes. "Let me know when you're finished by looking up at me, don't talk about what you wrote for now." When all but a few group members have finished, I say, "Those of you who aren't finished, why don't you just finish the sentence you're writing and then come back to the group?"

Back in the group, I ask each person to read his story aloud, still in the role of his fantasy.

Discussion: This task, like the verbal childhood memory exercise discussed earlier, especially facilitates a recall of childhood experiences. The work that follows can capitalize on this by taking specific situations suggested by the stories or by continuing with further childhood group activities such as role-playing school or play scenes. Once the task has been learned, it can be used for further warm-ups or continued group work. For example, group members can be encouraged to write letters to one another, to write about their families, to finish sentences in writing, always with the comment: "Try to let your hand do the writing for you."

Psychodrama is a way of playing. Left-handed writing is a very direct way to the child in each of us. It never ceases to amaze me that a room full of worried-looking, self-conscious, wary "grown-ups" can so readily be transformed. Body postures and facial expressions change as each person concentrates first on thinking about his childhood and then on the task of writing in this new way. People sit on the floor, sprawl, looking comfortable and absorbed. The stories are usually simple in language, very different from the way we usually talk. "I'm Cathy. I am five. I have a big brother and a big dog. I want to go to school but they won't let me." "My name is Bob. I like to run fast. School is lousy." "Dear Mary: I'm mad at you. You hurt my feelings. Goodbye forever. Love, Tom." In hospital wards, where the isolation of each patient is almost palpable at times, left-handed writing often serves as a bridge between people. Our adult selves are experts at distancing others; as children we can reach out.

4. The blind walk, an encounter technique.

Directions: After having people choose partners and pick the number 1 or 2, I say, "I would now like all the 1's to close their eyes and the 2's to lead them around this room. See how much rapport you can establish with your partner. Those of you who are leading might concentrate on giving your partner as full an experience of this environment as you can. The possibilities are plentiful. You can touch, but don't talk at all." After 5 minutes, the procedure is repeated with partners reversing roles.

Discussion: The warm-up can end here with everyone coming back to the circle and, one pair at a time, having a dialogue with his partner about the experience. This is an experience involving trust. The dialogues will be relevant to each person's ability to trust. Further work can involve doubling and role-reversing and can then be expanded to include other situations reminiscent of this one. For example, suppose Bob says to Tom, "I liked leading you but when you were leading me I tightened up, I just couldn't get myself to trust you."

Eva: Who else could you say that sentence to?

Bob: . . .'When you were leading me I couldn't get myself to trust you?'. . . My wife, I guess. We're always arguing about how I have to be boss all the time.

Eva: Can you choose someone in the group to take the role of your wife? O.K. Start by saying the sentence to her, and Joan, just respond by fitting yourself into this situation.

The blind walk has many variations, some or all of which can be used in warm-ups. All should take 5–10 minutes and be done by both partners in both roles.

(1) "This time you can talk but not touch. Stay close to your partner and give him a verbal picture of what he is about to encounter, for example, 'You can take 3 steps for-

ward, then you'll be close to a chair. Walk around the chair.' Again give your partner as full an experience as possible of this environment. I will be making some changes in the way the room is set up so that there will be some unfamiliarity for all of you." I then set up various obstacles: 2 rows of chairs back to back to make a narrow path, a stack of chairs as a tower, some overturned chairs, etc., changing these again as the partners change roles.

(2) "Now I'd like you to try something very difficult. I'd like you to keep a distance of at least 3 feet from your partner and I'd like the leaders to encourage the followers to take risks. There's running, jumping, exploring new aspects of the room, skipping, etc. Keep your distance from your partner. I will be making some changes in the way the room is set up so that it will be unfamiliar in places."

(3) "Both partners close their eyes. Touch but don't talk."

(4) "Both partners close their eyes. Talk but don't touch."

(5) "Shut your eyes and explore the room by yourself."

Blind walk variations 2–5 should be attempted only after one of the first two versions has been done. The last two can be quite anxiety-provoking and should be timed accordingly; 2–3 minutes may be enough.

If more than one version of these walks is done—as a prelude to a day-long workshop, for example—spontaneity and playfulness usually increase with each task. If this is not the case and the group becomes more restricted and constrained, the warm-up can be discontinued with the constraint as the focus of further role-playing.

5. Family sculptures, a technique developed by Virginia Satir.

Directions: "I would like to try something new today. We haven't done it before so no one knows how to do it. It's called 'family sculpture' and means that I want you to give us a living picture of your family. Would you like to try it, John?" I pick John because he has indicated conflicts with his mother and father in the last session. If the group is very unspontaneous or new to me, I may ask a staff member to volunteer, or I may sculpt my own parents, using members of the group. If John agrees, I continue, "How many people are there in your family? Could you pick someone to be your father, mother, etc.? All right. Now I'd like you to sculpt these people into a picture that would tell me something about the way your family relates. If I were walking along in the park and saw your sculpture, what would it look like? What picture would I get? Family members, your only job is to be putty in John's hands. Don't talk, and let John mold you into a sculpture. John, don't tell them how you want them to look. Place them where you want them and mold their bodies into the right position; you can even mold their facial expressions. Good. Now put yourself into the sculpture." If John has difficulty understanding, some examples can be given. "You know, some people sculpt their father with his back to the family and Mom and the children huddling close together. Or you could put Dad down on the floor with Mom standing over him, ruling the roost. There are all kinds of possibilities."

After John has finished, I say to the group members, "Be sure you each get a look at this sculpture. If you can't see it from where you're sitting, come on over here and take a look at each family member. Family members, hold your pose for another minute or so, then you can relax."

Discussion: When this task is used for a warm-up, there are all kinds of possibilities. One is to ask each family member to say a sentence that would fit the way he or she felt in the sculpture. Then group members can say a sentence for John, guessing how it might feel to be part of his family. Further work on John's family could follow, or a theme can be picked up from the group and tried out on various group members. For example, the theme might be isolation. Several people may comment, "I can't seem to touch or see anyone in this family." The theme can be pursued with each, asking whether the statement would fit for his own family and then setting up a scene with the family member(s) to whom he would like to say it.

Another way of working, especially if the group is scheduled for more than one hour, would be to encourage the rest of the group members to sculpt their families, reserving the decision about what to work on until the group has seen all the sculptures. If people are reluctant to sculpt their families, it is of course possible to use any other theme for a sculpture: "Sculpt a person that you get along with in the group in the attitude you most like to see him. Sculpt one of the staff members in a way that really bugs you. Sculpt me in the way you see me operating in the group and then yourself in relation to me."

Sculpting is very rewarding. It immediately accomplishes several goals: getting group members off their seats, permitting a nonthreatening form of touch, giving the sculptor a feeling of having some control in a situation—the family—in which he has often felt quite helpless. The sculpture also presents sculptor, family, and group members with rich themes for further work.

6. Nonverbal conversations.

Directions: After dividing the room in half, I ask the members to have a nonverbal conversation with someone on the other side of the room, using the way the conversation is going to decide whether to move closer or remain at a distance.

Discussion: This is an unusual, somewhat threatening task to groups who are unprepared for the experiential techniques. It should not be attempted with a new, shy group. Staff member participation is helpful in providing some modeling for the group as it starts.

This warm-up is very helpful when an ongoing group has been excessively verbal or intellectualizing in its responses. The task provides welcome relief from an excess of verbiage. It leads to a discussion in which nonverbal messages are the focus. The work that follows often has a more direct, vivid quality.

7. Machines. Both this and the next technique come to us from the theater.

Directions: After breaking up the group into teams of 5, I ask each group to take a moment and assign the numbers 1, 2, 3, 4, or 5 to each member. I then pick a team to start the activity and say, "O.K., now I'd like number 1 to come to the center of the room and begin a movement that could be part of a machine. Don't talk about it, just do it. Mystify us. You don't have to know what the machine is, just a mechanical movement. Fine. Now I'd like number 2 to come up and move in a way that relates to number 1 and makes sense in terms of creating a whole machine." I repeat the instructions for 3 and 4 and then ask number 5, still without talking, to make sense of the machine and come up and show us how to use it. I will then ask him to tell us in words what the machine was and what he was doing.

Discussion: This task tends to be successful in warming up a group which has been "too serious"—it is excellent for a group that needs to have fun and experience some spontaneous play. Further work will emerge from descriptions of the experience, associations to it, or fantasies aroused by the childlike quality of the task.

8. Nonverbal gift-giving.

Directions: The group stands in a circle. "I'm going to give the person next to me a gift. I'm not going to talk and there aren't any real presents. I am going to show something about the quality of the gift by my gesture and how I hand it to him. He will then receive my gift and give a gift of his own to the next person." If further instruction is needed, I say, "Use your imagination. You can pick a rose from a rose bush and hand it to your partner, or take some sticky gum off your shoe—anything goes. You can put the rose behind your ear, between your teeth or wear it as a corsage when you receive it, you can grind the gum into the floor, throw it away, or stick it on your own sole."

Discussion: This warm-up is seldom appropriate for a new group. It obviously would not function in a group where some hostilities have arisen among members. It is an excellent task for a group already acquainted with nonverbal communication in which enough familiarity exists to make gift-giving a natural occurrence.

The follow-up discussion usually produces poignant memories, which are easily used for further work, of other dreaded or welcomed gifts.

9. Stamping.
   Directions: The group stands in a circle. "We're going to try something really crazy today. First of all, I want you to stop talking and really get in touch with where and how you're standing. Get a little space around you. Get a good grip on the floor with your feet. Loosen your knees so you're free to move if you want to. Now, try stamping your feet. Stamp as hard as you can. Harder. If you want to make noise with it, go ahead. Are you worrying about the other people watching you? They aren't. They're either stamping or worrying themselves. See if you can forget everything but the stamping. Good."
   Discussion: This exercise can only be performed if the people downstairs will put up with it. (We were once caught by an angry druggist whose pharmacy was right below us; he insisted that we had made several bottles jump from the shelves.) It is valuable in bringing some life back into a dead, tired group and encourages comments about expressing aggressive, hostile behavior which are useful for further work.

Psychodrama demands that we play with children heavily burdened by their grown-up disguises. The atmosphere in our groups is usually rational, often serious, abstract, and wary. The group members are self-conscious grown-ups fearing the failures they were warned against by their parent grown-ups. The program calls for them to keep cool, calm, and collected; to know better; to think before they talk; to be mature; to do things right—stifling thoughts; thoughts which throttle spontaneity. The leader, the clown in the circus of psychotherapy, uses the warm-up as a way of giving permission to be spontaneous. To flop, to be silly, to shout, to cry. To remind the grown-ups that a neglected child exists inside each of them.

Chapter 4

The Double

This technique is referred to as "alter ego" by some directors. Like most of the concepts in this book, it originates with Moreno. For me it has become psychodrama's most vital technique, the one with the most varied uses and—if I had to choose—the most powerful one. The double is a person who stands behind the protagonist and acts out another aspect of his dilemma. He will usually act out something implicit in the situation but not available to the protagonist.

John, for example, wants to work on why he is such a pushover with his boss. We ask him to confront his boss and find that, in the dialogue, he is timid and soft-spoken, easily ignored. We give him a double who acts out his inner fury, shouts at the boss, threatens to quit—shows our protagonist in a dramatic fashion that there is an alternative way of behaving. Doubling is a unique method of communicating the nature of conflict. It is also one of the most effective pathways for the expression of empathy. To double is to "put oneself in the other's place."

When I was a child I developed a game which turned out to form the basis of my doubling. When looking at pictures of old masters, I would assume the physical position and facial expression of persons in the painting. *If I were carrying a spear and my hands were tense around it, my eyes wide open and eyebrows raised, what would I feel? Or, in my velvet gown, my hands idly playing with the lace on my blouse, my eyes cast down—what am I thinking about the man who is looking over my shoulder?*

Our language contains many phrases and metaphors expressing the essence of doubling: *If I were you . . . put yourself in my place . . . put yourself in my shoes.* We each want the other to know what we experience, and we're infinitely curious about the inner life of the other. One of the most frustrating aspects of human existence is the fact that we can only show a small aspect of an experience at any given time— only the top of the iceberg shows. We've become so accustomed to our partial vision that often we're not even aware of the rest. Again, the language is filled with a phrasebook of these frustrations: *Dr. Jekyll and Mr. Hyde . . . only a bird in a gilded cage . . . putting on a good face . . . still waters run deep . . . shallow brooks are noisy.* When we attempt to explore the inner life of the other person in conversation, we find ourselves brought up short by conventions which allow only the most superficial excursions. *I know how you must feel . . . I've felt that way myself . . . I know . . . I've been there.* How do you know? What way did you feel? Where have you been? Alas, the answers are available only in the rarest of circumstances. Doubling provides a means of producing the inner life, of talking—as we shall see—on several levels at the same time.

To varying degrees, each of us is aware of conflicts, dualities, hypocrisies. And yet we are often bound to represent only one side at a time. We play roles in which we are either brave *or* scared, moral *or* sinful, good *or* bad, angry *or* kind. We seem magically to believe that if we were to let in a conflicting feeling, if we were to give it expression, all would be lost. *If I see someone caught in a fire, I can save him—but I mustn't remember that I'm afraid of fire, too. If I did, I might not be able to act, and if I were to say I'm scared, my chance to be heroic would be lost.* We often suppress emotions which might interfere with something we expect of ourselves. *A good mother does not show frustration or anger. Men don't cry.* Further, we want to avoid becoming vulnerable to the other. And so we hide tenderness or caring. *Play hard to get, stay cool, give him the cold shoulder.* The more important the hidden emotion is to our inner life, the more likely its suppression contributes to the formation of symptoms. Doubling is a way to begin to give voice to the conflict within us.

The double is the inner voice. The voice of conflict, of self-pity, of irony. The double is the coward inside the hero, the saint inside the sinner, the needy child in the lonely eccentric. The double takes a chance on losing control by raising the possibilities of tears, rage, tenderness. The double can raise his voice. The double can laugh.

Doubling presents endless possibilities and because of that, we must use this technique cautiously. Doubling is not an avenue for the expression of one's own emotions *unless* they fit the person for whom one is doubling. The person who doubles must pay close attention to the cues given by the protagonist. He is there to help the protagonist become aware of conflictual feelings, to help him see alternative ways of expressing emotions. If the protagonist gives consistent signs of rejecting the double and it becomes clear that what the double is saying is not relevant, the double must be willing to be flexible—to let go his precious hunch and try something else. (More of this in the section, "The stubborn double.")

There is one other caution. Doubling is a very powerful technique. When a double is successful, she is experienced by the protagonist as an inner voice, as a catalyst—not as another person. For this reason, our protagonist often drops the defenses she uses normally. If our protagonist were asked by her mother, for example, or even by a close friend, "Do you sometimes want to murder your husband?" she'd probably pooh-pooh the idea, saying of course she gets angry, like anyone else, but murder, ridiculous! If, on the other hand, our protagonist is confronting someone who role-plays her husband in a scene, and one of the usual endless arguments breaks out, and she hears her double saying, "I feel so frustrated I could kill you. I've thought of it before. I really could kill you," she may well agree with her double and then become frightened of the intensity of her feeling. The double facilitates the expression of feelings which are often frightening and unpleasant for the protagonist. It is important for the double to be aware of this possibility and to include it in her doubling. She may want to say, after our protagonist has agreed she could murder, "Now I've said it. And I'm really scared. I didn't think I was that kind of a person," or to ask "Did I scare myself? Did I go too far?" Both the group leader and the double need to be aware of the frequent defenselessness of the protagonist. The double must carefully judge the protagonist's reactions to her doubling and be prepared to either comment on them or change the course of her doubling if necessary. The leader must be prepared to find ways of giving the protagonist more control—to interrupt the scene, ask for the protagonist's feelings, send in another double with an opposite point of view, encourage the protagonist to argue with her doubles. Unless this kind of caution is observed, the danger is that the protagonist feels manipulated into saying something she wasn't ready to say.

New members of ongoing groups usually learn to double by watching others. Doubling is a very natural technique and needs little in the way of explanation. In a new group, or with a new member of an ongoing group—let's call her Jane—I usually start by asking Jane whether she will accept a double. When she asks what that is, I try to be very brief in my reply, emphasizing that "doubling is a great deal easier to do than to explain," stating that I'd like to ask Carol to double for Jane in order to say some of the things Jane may think but not say. I may add some of the following sentences: "You know, you can argue with your double or you can agree. It's just the way it goes in our minds sometimes—two sides going at each other. If you feel your double is barking up the wrong tree, be sure to tell her so and tell her why. She may still keep going, but tell her anyhow." I have found the latter to be an important instruction because there often seems to be a misunderstanding on the part of the protagonist that the double is going to "tell the truth" about her. When the doubles are played by psychiatrists, nurses, or other mental health personnel, it is important for the protagonist to know that she does not have to accept what is being said, lest the doubling degenerate into a kind of mental health brainwashing.

I then make it clear that our rule is that only Jane can hear her doubles. Others in the scene with Jane cannot reply to what the doubles say. If Jane wants to say a sentence said by one of her doubles to someone else in the scene, she has to repeat it herself. This rule is very important to me because it (1) helps reduce confusion and (2) provides a way for Jane to take responsibility for herself and to make clear what she is willing to say at a given time. The confusion which can result from the argument of two people, each with a double, if the double's voice can be countered by the other person and his double, is often overwhelming.

Further, the double may be able to say something Jane can't and this deprives Jane of an opportunity to say it herself. Jane is demure while her double tells her husband that she's sick to death of him. Occasionally, by a victorious smile, Jane lets us know that her double is "right on." In order to face her hostile feelings, Jane will need to go one step further than to shyly acknowledge her double: she will have to say the words herself. On the other hand, Jane may not feel the hostile feelings her double attributes to her, or may not be ready to face them. In that case, it is important for her to be able to talk to her double, telling her "But I'd never talk to my husband that way. He's been so good to me. Anyway, I don't talk that way," and have her double retreat for the time being.

I make one other rule in the beginning. The rule is that both the double and Jane always use the first person. If the double sees something Jane is doing and says, "You're twiddling your thumbs," she is no longer her double but a person outside of Jane, observing her. If she says, "I'm twiddling my thumbs," she can be perceived as a part of Jane, encouraging Jane to talk further about it. If Jane then answers, "No, you're wrong, I was scratching my other hand," she has again lengthened the distance between herself and her double, making her double the other "you," not the self. Even in the case of such a seemingly minor disagreement, I insist that Jane keep using "I" as she talks with her double: "No, why would I twiddle my thumbs? I was just scratching my hand." It is very important to keep Jane and Carol from thinking of each other as two opposing forces. They're both Jane. Jane may have internal disagreements, questions. But she's asking herself, not somebody else. When the double is used correctly, Jane is hardly aware of her. She simply uses her to express her own feelings. In order for this to occur, the double must talk in such a way that she can be accepted by Jane. She can't talk simultaneously with Jane or anyone else because then Jane won't be able to hear her. She must listen closely to Jane in order to find the right times in which to speak.

If Jane agrees to let Carol double for her, I usually ask Carol to be slightly to the side of and slightly behind Jane, and to assume a similar physical position. It is important for Carol to be near enough to Jane so that she can easily perceive Jane's physical reactions. And it is important that Carol and Jane are not face-to-face, since this position seems to enhance the feeling of oppositeness, of two separate people. When Carol, the double, is behind and slightly to the side of Jane, she can more easily be perceived as an inner voice. From Carol's point of view, the scene may go something like this:

Double: (I'm Jane's double. Now what? How will I know what to do? I don't know what she's thinking. Jane's physical position tells me something about her. Let's see. She's sitting down. I'll sit down. She's crossed her legs; so will I. She's beating a tattoo on the floor with her left foot; I'm doing it. I feel impatient. Maybe that's what she feels. I'll give it a try.) I'm feeling impatient. I want this to start.

Jane: (says nothing but nods her head in vigorous assent).

Double: (This is the beginning. Now Jane and her husband are arguing. He is riding her about all the money she spends at the shrink's. What a bastard. That's how I feel but she's just sitting there. Tapping her foot again now. I know why she's impatient.) I wish he'd stop talking. I'm so sick of this kind of talk. But I feel guilty, too. So I just sit here.

Jane (ignoring double): Well, what can I do? I really don't feel right about using the money you earn for extravagances.

Double: (Oh, that Jane! No guts at all. Maybe I can goad her into speaking up for herself.) I do feel right about using the money. I just haven't got the guts to say so. And I'm mad at him for bringing it up all the time. And I don't have the guts to say that either. *(Jane doesn't say anything. She looks like she might cry. I'm too mad at her to feel sorry. I continue.)*

Double: I'm almost crying because it's the same thing over and over again.

Jane: It's true. I don't know what to do about it.

Double: I'm sitting here the way I always do and you're talking on and on the way you always do and I want to tell you how I'm feeling for a change.

Jane: Well, I do feel hurt because you seem to criticize me so much.

Double: There, I said it. *(I'm not mad at her anymore. She isn't experiencing anger. She's hurt and she did say so. She doesn't have that trapped, impatient look anymore. I like that. She seems more real now. They continue the scene. Jane practices saying something of what she's been feeling. Her husband hears her. I am needed a lot less as the scene finishes. I feel satisfied with how it went.)*

Some Styles of Doubling

The colorless double. This type of doubling is very close to the process of individual therapy. The double is there to understand the protagonist, to validate what he has to say by putting it just a bit more strongly, and to give him opportunities to look at some different choices he has in this situation, mostly by asking questions.

Florence: I want to keep staying at my parents' house and they want me there too.
Double: They really do like it when I'm there.
Florence: Yes, they make such a fuss you'd think I was still in my teens.
Double: Sometimes I feel like I'm still in my teens when I stay with them.
Florence: It's true. It's hard to feel grown up in the house where you were a kid.
Double: Have I felt like a kid lately?
Florence: Yes *(pause)*.
Double: How do they make me feel like a kid?
Florence: It's not their fault, it's just the way it is. Mom always watched over everybody and she still does.
Double: Good old Mom. Always watching. Does it bug me some of the time?
Florence: Yes, but there's no point in telling her.

The double does not emerge as a vivid aspect of Florence's personality. Rather, this double blends in with Florence, leading a bit here and there, but always strictly within the framework of Florence's words. If this double has a hunch about something that Florence is not saying, she would wait until Florence said something relevant and then ask a question. If Florence disagrees, the double will drop the argument. This is of course the most supportive—and, at the same time, the least dramatic—use of doubling. A patient who has difficulty accepting what another person says about him or one who is frightened that the double will be able to "read his mind" will have the least difficulty with this type of doubling. Anyone unused to having a double and who is showing some signs of anxiety can be reassured with these techniques. The patient who flatly denies the double's statements and uses them to fall out of role ("That isn't right, that isn't what I'd think at all") can work more successfully with a colorless double than with other types of doubling.

The satirical double. This double—very much suited to my own style—is rendered effective by a quality that often deadens a psychodrama: the colorless, flat quality of the protagonist. The satirical double can exaggerate Florence's slow, quiet way of talking in order to get her to see what she is doing. Style is very important here. This type of doubling requires a light touch and enough sensitivity to stop and adopt a more serious style when necessary. I have to be at ease with my sense of humor before I can use it therapeutically. If I inhibit what I'm doing because I think Florence will be hurt or embarrassed, she'll sense my inhibition. We will get stymied. On the other hand, I may be comfortable enough with myself to go ahead, knowing that Florence might be miffed, but in the hope that our process will provide a stimulus for greater self-awareness.

Florence: There's not any point in telling my mom that it bugs me when she waits up for me all hours of the night. She'd still do it.
Double: There's no point in telling mom anything.
Florence: Well, I wouldn't want to hurt her feelings.
Double: I'm a very good girl. I don't hurt people's feelings.
Florence: It's true. I've just never been the kind of person who could just speak up and say anything.
Double: I'm too good.
Florence: I don't mean it that way.
Double: I don't even have any bad thoughts. At least not about my mother.
Florence: Oh, shut up!
Double: She's really getting to me now! I'm going to see if I can get out of this. But what if I hurt my double's feelings?
Florence: No, I'm not worrying about that. *(Laughs.)*
Double: What do I want to say to my mom about the other night?
Florence: I'd like her to just leave me alone more. Let me come and go as I wish.

The satirical double uses exaggeration in a good-natured attempt to bring the emotions or defenses into awareness. John

says, "I don't think I could even talk to my wife about this."
His double says, "I'd probably disappear," or "I'm really
weak" (slumping in his chair in an attitude of total weakness),
or "My God! I might get angry and then she might get angry
and then what?"

Mary complains about her loneliness. Her double may say,
"No one else has ever felt like this. This is really unique.
Because this is the kind of loneliness you can't do anything
about." Or, "I certainly wasn't going to call anybody to talk
about this. That would have spoiled it."

John says, "I've given up telling my kids what to do. They're
over 18. They're on their own." His double says, "Now I just
tell them how I expect them to run their lives. I don't tell them
what to do. Just Dan, about not burning his draft card, and I
want John to work with me, and I don't think Jane is ready to
get married. That's all."

The most important aspect of satirical doubling is the double's willingness to be flexible. Many people are likely to be
upset by a satirical approach. The double must keep in touch
enough to know when to stop. The leader can, of course, be of
help by encouraging John to fight with his double if he doesn't
like what he's saying, asking John whether he understands the
group's laughter and, if not, to ask what it was about, etc.
When successful, the satirical double often opens the door to
some change or shift in a person's position. It's hard to continue doing the same thing seriously once you've laughed at
yourself in public. You're in this group where they're all supposed to be serious about their problems and everybody's
laughing. Maybe it's not so bad as all that.

The passionate double. Psychodrama is a way to help people
express emotions. Often, the protagonist betrays intense, passionate emotion by her tension, body posture, or the tremor in
her voice. But her actual conversation betrays very little of
this. Her voice is quiet, her words colorless, her body posture
rigid. The double is free to express the strong emotions. Here,
as with the satirical double, the double also exaggerates, but
not in an attempt to ridicule. Rather, the intent is to teach an

alternative solution, a solution involving emotional expression. The cautions are many. The therapist's personal feelings about the expression of strong emotion are most important. If I can't tolerate the expression of strong emotion, I'll be pretending or "hamming" in using this technique and will distance, rather than teach. Secondly, it is important that I don't become so wound up in my portrayal that I forget that I'm doubling for someone else. It is still very important to check with the protagonist and to use any opportunity which may help her express the emotion herself.

Florence: I'd like my mother to leave me alone more. Let me come and go as I wish.
Double: I want her off my back! I'm sick of being watched!
Florence: She doesn't mean it that way.
Double: I know she doesn't mean it that way but I feel it that way. Christ, why do I have to worry about her all the time! She does what *she* wants to do.
Florence: I'd like to tell her to stop being so nosy.
Double: I'd like to tell her I'm *sick* of it. But I'm afraid.
Florence: Why am I so scared to get mad at her?
Double: Why? Why? It's easier to think about that than to get mad at her, that's for sure. And I am really angry. *(Yelling.)* I'm sick and tired of being treated like a little kid!
Florence (breaking out of the scene and looking at the leader): I wish I could talk that way. *(Laughs.)*

At this point, coordination between the leader and the double is very important. The leader now asks Florence to pick someone to play the role of her mother. (If this process looks like it may take long enough to break the dramatic tension, the leader may wish to pick someone to play Florence's mother.)

Leader: Here's your mother, Florence. How about trying to say some of the stuff that's hard for you to say. Use whatever your double said that fits and say it to your mother.

The double also stays in the scene and continues to model strong emotional responses for Florence. The rule that only

Florence can hear her double is important in forcing Florence to repeat those sentences she'd like to say herself.

The passionate double reduces conflicts to their bare essentials. John wants to talk about the "relationship" between himself and his wife. Jack, doubling for him, tells her: "You don't love me," or "I've hated you for years," or "I'm jealous of the kids," or "I love you and I want you and I think you're going to leave me."

Jane tells her husband, "Our trouble is that we don't communicate." Mary doubles for her and says: "You haven't talked to me about anything but business in 15 years," or "I can't stand your silence another day. Sometimes I think I'll scream just to get some noise into the house!" or "I don't even think you know who I am anymore. You and the boys and fishing, me and the girls and PTA, and money. That's all we talk about. Who are you?"

John says, "I think we've drifted apart." His double Jack says, "I don't think you want me to touch you anymore," or "You're cold with me. I'm scared of you."

Jane says, "I think we've drifted apart." Mary, her double, says, "You don't see me as a woman anymore. I'm the lady that talks to you at breakfast and dinner and keeps your house and your children clean. I want you to hold me."

Mother says, "My children are members of the new generation. I don't understand them." Her double says: "I've failed with them. They're all crazy and they'll come to no good." Or, "They don't appreciate me. After all I've done for them. And now I'm all alone and they don't care." Or, "I'm furious with those kids. They use the house, my money, my car. And I let them. I'd like to throw those leeches out, them and all their friends."

Love. Anger. Tenderness. Self-pity. Protectiveness. Fear of death. Fear. Sadly enough, these emotions often become the subtext of a superficially banal conversation; they are betrayed only by a gesture, a breath quickly drawn, an "inappropriate" tear. The double's role is to bring the subtext to the surface. The advantage in this type of doubling is that John's and Mary's cues are easy to read. We want to be known. If my double is on the right track, I'm rooting for her to keep it up. If she's wrong, I tell her right away or I don't respond or I get bored. But it's really good when she's saying something I need to say.

In teaching this kind of doubling, the greatest difficulty I have encountered is our cultural training against being "emotional." People who are free enough, open enough, loud enough, and soft enough to express strong emotions are hard to find. People who consider the latter uncool, corny, or soap-operatic (depending on the age group) abound.

The oppositional double. Whenever our protagonist makes a strong statement—especially when protesting too much emotion—the double argues the opposite point just as vehemently.

Florence: I hate my parents.
Double: I love my parents, they take care of me.

Florence: I'm tired of my boyfriend. I'm going to tell him I can't take his drinking anymore.
Double: I love him. At least he lets me take care of him. No one else does.

Florence: I'm not going to drink anymore. I know now that it's just stupid. I have to confront my problems.
Double: I can't confront my problems. They're too terrible. I know I'll drink some more.

Sometimes this technique is used with two doubles:

Florence: I don't know what I'll do when my mother-in-law arrives.
Double 1: I'll tell her to leave.
Double 2: I'll tell her to stay.
Florence: I just can't face her. I'll leave a message with one of the kids.
Double 1: That'll get her!
Double 2: But what if I hurt her feelings and she gets upset?

The main point, of course, is to surprise Florence: to confront her with feelings which she does not usually admit, to show her alternatives, to entice her into conducting arguments she never thought possible. With this technique it is very important for the leader to encourage Florence to argue with her double, lest the scene be one-sided and Florence simply let her double talk on, without facing any of the conflicts implicit in her ambivalence.

Physicalizing the double. Just as body language can be used as a way to gather information about how it feels to be the protagonist, the double's body language can show the protagonist another part of himself. Most often, the double gets her cues from Florence, our perennial protagonist. If there is any inconsistency between what she says and how her body looks, I may dramatize her body language as I double for her.

Florence (sitting very stiffly, hardly moving a muscle in her face as she talks): I like people. I always have.

Double (copying and exaggerating the nonverbal cues): I like people but I don't like them to come very close. I don't let them see very much of me.

Florence: That's not true. I have very good friends.

Double (in a monotone voice): It's just that if I moved my face it might upset them. (I know that Florence alternates between a show of great bravery and independence and total collapse—to the extent that she needs periodic hospitalization, and I use this information to make a point.)

Florence: I've learned a lot here and I think I'm going to be alright this time.

Double (looking very weak, slouched down in the chair, speaking in a small voice): But what about me? Who's going to take care of me when I get nervous?

Florence: Come on, I'm not so nervous anymore.

Double (leaning over and grasping Florence's hand): I feel really helpless, somebody has to do something for me.

Florence (undoing the double's hands, beginning to laugh): Come on, take care of yourself, you baby.

Double: But I'm the baby part of Florence. I need somebody *(clasping Florence's hand and sliding onto the floor, hanging on to her in an obvious attempt to drag her down).*

Florence: Look, you can stand up on your own two feet. *(She disentangles herself and looks around the group, helpless, exasperated, amused.)*

Group members and the leader encourage her to fight her double, who has started to drag her down again. The struggle continues. Florence wins. Florence's physical victory over her double is cheered in the group. This is one instance where I do not insist that both double and protagonist use the form "I." It is clear that the double is playing a specific part of Florence, a part with which Florence is in great conflict. If this conflict takes the "I'm trying to get rid of you" form, it is realistic enough. There is no doubt that Florence is struggling with a part of herself.

I do not use this type of doubling with strangers. Florence needs to know me and my good intentions thoroughly before I expect her to enter into such a struggle. If she loses, she hears me saying, "I guess I'm not so strong after all, I can't even get this double of mine on her feet." Winning isn't easy because I'm stubborn, too, just as stubborn as she is in her helplessness when she first came to the hospital. The struggle is outrageously theatrical. Both double and protagonist have to be willing to risk the ludicrous. My goal is to anchor the message in Florence's body. Once she has actually struggled with this helpless part of herself it's harder to forget it, or to forget that she is strong. If Florence is depressed, engaging her in this battle is an almost certain temporary cure. It's hard to stay depressed when your blood's rushing through your head, your breath is coming fast, and the crowd is cheering you on to victory. This is an exercise in trust. Florence must accept me as representing a part of herself—that is necessary for any doubling—but she must also trust me not to hurt her or be hurt by her physically. There are no guarantees; that's why it's a trust exercise.

The double as counselor. Often, psychodrama grants a magic wish: "If I only could have thought then what I think now. If I only could have told him that then. If I only could have thought of it then, but I was too caught up in the argument." Psychodrama affords time out right in the middle of an argument. Florence and Fred are going at it:

Florence: You do this to me one more time and I'm leaving.

Fred: You mean you'd leave me over a little thing like coming home late because I had to work overtime?

Florence: Oh no you don't! I'm not going to get caught arguing with you again. You know it isn't the first time! We've argued about this over and over again.

Florence's double: There I go, caught right in the argument I wanted to avoid.

Leader: Florence, why don't you take some time out with your double to think about what you want to do next. Maybe you two could walk around together, talking about this situation. Fred, could you just wait while they do this? I'll give you and your double a chance to do the same later.

Florence: It's true, I always say I'm not going to argue and then I do.

Double: What do I really want?

Florence: I want him to apologize.

Double: That's what I want him to do, what do I want?

Florence: I want him to see I'm right.

Double: What do I want? What am I feeling?

Florence: I feel so hurt.

Double: Could I tell him that?

At this point the leader asks Florence to talk to Fred again, starting the scene on a new level.

The main objective of the double as counselor is to disentangle the protagonist from whatever games are going on in the argument, from "winning or losing" since, chances are, both mean losing, and to help her become aware of the pain which underlies all the quick repartee. The message given by this type of doubling is, of course, that one can take time out, that real feelings can be stated, that the argument does not have to continue at the same level. Once learned with a double, the mechanism can often be used in the actual situation.

The collective double. There are many times—the best times in psychodrama—when the whole audience becomes involved with the conflicts of those working on a scene. I can see they are taking sides. In the center of the room, Joan is accusing her husband, Hal, of being unwilling to change, unwilling to respond to her emotionally. She is crying. I look at the other people in the group, totaling about 25. Many of the men are showing physical signs of anger. Teeth are clenched, jaws set, fists clenched. The women on the other hand, look frustrated and outraged. Some are raising their brows in an exasperated expression. They are looking at each other and nodding in sympathy. Joan just can't seem to get her point across, but *they* understand. They've been there. When the scene between Joan and Hal has gone as far as it can go, one of my options is to let the group join in a "collective double." I usually begin by commenting on what I've observed.

Leader: People seemed really involved in what Joan and Hal were doing. I saw a lot of you change your facial expressions and react physically to what was going on. For now, I don't want you to talk *about* what you were feeling. I'd like you, instead, to put yourself in Joan or Hal's place. As Joan or Hal, what would you like to say right now? Start by saying who you are and then say what you feel needs saying. 'I'm Joan and I just don't know what's happening,' for example. People usually join in easily. 'I'm Joan and it seems so obvious that I show all the emotion in this family.' . . . 'I'm Joan and I'd like to get you into a good argument because at least it would show you're alive.' . . . 'I'm Hal and I'm tired of your nagging.' . . . 'I'm Hal and I can't do anything right.'

Some men begin to take the woman's part and vice versa. John says, "I'm Joan and I really feel stuck, I'm doing the best I can and everyone is down on me." Mary says, "I'm Hal and I'm afraid. I'm really angry and if I let that stuff out I don't know what I'd do."

While the group is doubling, I have to assess Joan's and Hal's ability to listen. If the scene has left them frustrated and confused, and if either one of them is the kind of person whose confusion quickly builds to a paranoid feeling (*None of them understands, they're all against me*), then I may want to limit the time of the collective double, or I may want to add some controls for Hal and Joan. I may tell them, before we begin, that I'd like them to just listen to the others for awhile, but that listening might become difficult and, if it does, to let us know that. I may simply watch their faces and stop to ask them to comment if I notice a strong reaction. Or I may make a rule that Hal or Joan say a sentence in response to each of their doubles. The collective double cannot continue unless Hal or Joan has commented. In this way, Hal and Joan can let out their reactions as they occur, rather than storing them up as evidence to be used against the group, and the overwhelming cumulative effect of a dozen different Joans and Hals is avoided.

If Hal and Joan seem to me to be individuals who can tolerate some of the ambiguity and confusion arising from the collective double, I ask them not to comment while the doubling is going on, just to listen. The group can then let off steam, building on each other's comments to say many of the things that they have held back during the scene with Hal and Joan, and during their own lives with their own spouses.

When the doubling is over, there are several options. If Hal and Joan have not been commenting, I always ask them to do so at this point. It is important for them to have a chance now to express some of the feelings they've held back during the collective double—a one-way conversation always builds up a good deal of frustration in the listener. I want to know what it was like to have so many doubles. If I find out that it was upsetting, I'll want to work now on Hal or Joan's feelings of being misunderstood by the group. If I find out that it was interesting or exciting, I'll want to know what Hal or Joan learned, what or who particularly touched them. I may then want to go back to working with Hal and Joan, starting a new dialogue with the sentence that Hal learned from the collective double.

I often use the collective double as a way of arriving at some closure after a difficult scene. No matter how ill-matched the people, how tenaciously stubborn the fighters, how well-rehearsed the conflicts, the group's expectation of a psychodrama is that there will be a resolution and "they will live happily ever after." (More about this in the chapter on closure.) However, in actuality, the scene often ends with an impasse. Hal and Joan, for example, continue the game ad infinitum; he is strong and silent, she rants and raves, neither looks like he's willing to give an inch. The frog remains a frog and the princess a princess. The group is frustrated and disappointed. In the collective double, each member of the group has a chance to vent his frustration in a way which is not directed against Hal and Joan or the group. John may be inclined to say, "Joan, why don't you lay off him? All you ever do is pick fights." This, needless to say, would nail us tightly into the middle of the blame frame; Joan would feel attacked and attack back and the hopelessness of the discussion would pervade the room. If on the other hand, John says, "I'm Hal and I just feel so attacked by Joan, I feel like she really wants to provoke me," the content is the same but Joan is not being attacked; instead Hal is being invited to deal with his feelings. John may be inclined to say, "This group isn't helping. They aren't getting any better." Obviously, this is a tempting pathway for each group member's frustrations: *It isn't that I'm not working at changing; it's that the group isn't helping me.* If John says instead, "I'm Hal and I feel like nothing's changing. We're just doing the same thing over and over again," the problem of responsibility for change is laid on Hal's own shoulders, where it belongs. The collective double serves to clear the air. People have a chance to say what they've been storing up. Once the feelings are out, there's less need to blame, to insist on magic solutions. We experience each other as people embroiled in complicated interactions which occur on many levels. We've each of us felt some of what Hal and Joan are stuck with. It isn't easy.

The stubborn double. All of the above methods of doubling can be used by the same person during the same scene—con-

secutively, interchangeably, what you will—and all of them
can be botched by the stubborn double. Nothing is worse than
the double who cannot take no for an answer.

> *Florence:* I'm sorry to see them leave.
> *Double:* I'm angry at them.
> *Florence:* I'm not angry at them. I'll miss them.
> *Double:* I'm really angry at them.
> *Florence:* I don't know, I just don't feel angry at them.
> *Double:* I still feel angry, really angry.
> *(Etc., etc.)*

This scene can obviously go on forever. If the double cannot
remember that it is of the utmost importance to be sensitive to
the protagonist, she may become a sort of psychological
saleslady, putting a great deal of pressure and strain on
Florence, who either does not have or is not ready to face the
feelings her double attributes to her.

Doubling is not leading. The double is there to help the pro-
tagonist become more aware of her feelings, her alternatives.
The double does not force her own individuality on the pro-
tagonist. The double takes her cues from the protagonist.
Florence could play her role in the scene without the double.
The double could not be in the role without Florence.

If I'm doubling for Florence I must be filled with questions:
*How would I feel if I were Florence? There. I said how I'd
feel. Is she accepting it? No? Should I give it one more try?
Was it a bored lack of acceptance or a passionate denial? If it's
the latter, I think I'll give it one more try. Is she tensing up? Is
she aware of it? Am I making her uncomfortable? Too much so
to keep working? Can I be quiet and see where she takes this
scene for a little while? Can I wait for her to give me the next
cue?* The more questions I can ask, the more material I gather
for doubling and the more I can remain flexible instead of
stubborn.

Doubling as an adjunct to therapy. Doubling is one of the
most flexible instruments of psychodrama. Its use is easily extended to the therapeutic scene. I have used doubling during

regular sessions of family and individual therapy. In thinking over my use of this technique with various patients, I find that I begin to use it most frequently for one of two reasons: either because someone is not talking, or because he's talking too glibly. In the first case, my questions are answered with silence; in the second, I find myself wishing for a quiet moment. In both instances, continuing to talk seems to make matters worse (until, of course, the initial defensive stance of the patient yields to more trust).

I had been seeing the Jones family for many weeks without making any headway with their 14-year-old daughter, Julie. While the rest of the family talked about problems they had with each other, or tried to talk about their problems with Julie to me, Julie just sat. She seemed alert and sensitive in her facial expressions, yet questions directed to her were usually answered with a sullen shrug of the shoulders—at most, a quick "yes" or "no." Needless to say, the family had originally come in because of their concern with Julie, who had got into considerable conflict with her parents over drugs.

For one of our sessions, the father had brought in a tape recording of Julie when she was allegedly on drugs and stated that he wished to play it for me. His tone was forbidding. I had the feeling that if he went through with this, Julie would never open her mouth in my office. I moved over to sit near her and said, "Julie, I have a hunch you want to say something to your dad about playing the tape." Julie, of course, shrugged her shoulders disdainfully. I continued, "Maybe we could do it together. I'd like to think out loud with you about the tape, first. I'll just be another part of you, OK?" Julie looked puzzled but didn't object.

"Let's see, I'm Julie," I said, beginning to double, "and Dad really brought the tape! I didn't think he'd go through with it. Wow! I am really mad. Doesn't he know I have feelings?"

Julie's eyes brightened a little.

I was a little worried about Julie's father. Would he see me as just taking his daughter's side against him? So far, he simply looked interested. I continued, "I'm really upset and when I'm upset I just can't talk. Especially not to *them*."

Julie nodded her head in surprise.

"Which doesn't mean I don't have anything to say. I really do want to tell Dad a thing or two about that tape, don't I?"

Julie nodded again, more vigorously.

Here's my chance, I thought to myself. "Could I take a chance on saying it even if he doesn't understand it? Just to get it off my own chest? What do I want to say to Dad?" There was a long pause; Julie looked at me, I gave her an encouraging look.

"You shouldn't have brought that tape, Dad."

Julie began to vent some of her anger. Thank goodness, the silent treatment was over. Dad, of course, moralized in his own defense, telling Julie he had made and brought the tape for her own good, because he only wanted to help her.

Again, I doubled for Julie, "See, talking doesn't do any good. I tell him I'm upset and he doesn't even hear me. He just goes on in the same old way. Why should I tell him anything? I don't think he knows I'm upset, even."

Julie showed me that these were her feelings.

I made another attempt to get her unstuck. "Could I ask him if he has any idea what I'm upset about?"

Again, Julie agreed.

Dad acknowledged her embarrassment. A beginning was made. During further sessions with the family, I used doubling not only with Julie, but with the parents as well.

The crucial aspect of the doubling technique in the above session was that it enabled me to get out of the "teenager versus grown-ups" game and to take a position which was recognizably empathetic to Julie without in any way patronizing her or, on the other hand, validating her symptoms. In talking with the family later, I found that my fear of her dad's resentment had been groundless. He had suffered Julie's silences so long that any answer from her—even if it was negative in feeling and coming to him via the therapist—was a relief.

My next example comes from individual therapy. During the few months I had been seeing Steven, each of us had changed his mind about the other. To begin with, I viewed him as an unusually literate, articulate young man, clever at setting intellectual traps for me in the first few sessions. Subtle allusions, tests of memory, tests of my ability to tolerate his liberal views—I had passed all of these with flying colors and we had spent the first few weeks feeling a delightful excitement. He was a smart patient, I was a smart therapist; we were well matched and enjoyed jockeying for position. Sadly enough, this phase lasted longer than I had expected. I found Steven quite reluctant to enter the realm of feelings. The closest we could get to his blocking of emotion was to talk about the trap he set himself: telling himself to go ahead and tell me something he was afraid of and then finding himself face-to-face with his complete distrust not only of me, but even of his own ability to recount the incident truthfully. There were traps within traps. I found that talking about this process wasn't enough; Steven continued to be dry and aloof during the interviews, unable to get in touch with what I suspected to be overwhelming feelings of loneliness and despair.

As we talked about his difficulties with his whiny, self-abnegating, mousy mother, it was obvious that he understood her problems and his own reactions to them—and that understanding wasn't enough. His discussion was devoid of feelings. I began to sense a kind of sneering contempt in his intellectualization and began to double.

Eva: If I'm you, I'm really bored with telling this story. I've told it to shrinks before. It never does any good, right?

Steven (laughs): Right.

Eva: I'm sick of my mother's whining and I'm sick of my own whining.

Steven: I don't whine. (*Steven objects strongly; I let him know by a nod of my head that I hear him.*)

Eva: I don't whine like she does, thank God for that. But I'm sick of talking about things. About her. It never does any good.

Steven: That's for sure.

Eva: I feel strongly about her but I don't show it.

Steven: I don't know what I feel. (*His mouth gets a stubborn look.*)

Eva: I really hate her.

Steven: It's true. I remember going into her bedroom and taking one of her favorite scarves and stuffing it in the garbage can. (*He is speaking with a great deal of vehemence now.*)

With Steven, doubling proved to be one of the only ways of getting away from his cold, abstract intellectualizations. For the rest of the hour, Steven was in touch with a part of himself he had locked away: the hate-filled little boy, afraid to talk back to his mother for fear of hurting her, yet filled with rage at her selfishness, her self-destructiveness, her weaknesses. We could now see some of the roots of his own lifelessness and his continuing fear of asserting his anger, especially with women.

Doubling is the heart of psychodrama. These techniques represent some of the ways I have used doubling in various settings. Our timid clinician will be able to use doubling as a bridge to further psychodrama techniques once he is willing to take the first step. The more he uses the technique, the more uses he'll find for it. Its limitations are the boundaries he sets for his personal growth.

Chapter 5

Role Reversal

We all play defensive games. When a conversation becomes potentially dangerous, when we feel we may be hurt or lose something, when we feel vulnerable to the other person, we take a stance: we act the injured party, we counterattack, we distract, we show physical signs of distress, we lecture. The defensive stance can take any number of forms; the point is, once it is taken, the conversation bogs down, any real exchange stops, and what follows becomes easily predictable. We are involved in a game.

John wants to tell Mary that he has been invited to be the speaker at the next meeting of his business associates. Mary, who feels that John has been drifting away from her and becoming more and more involved professionally, hears this as

61

a threat and defends herself by a sarcastic comment, "Well, there goes another weekend. Maybe I should write to your secretary and find out when you have a free evening." John's response is to withdraw by starting to read the newspaper. They are now playing the marital game "You Don't Love Me," rather than exchanging information about John's professional success. What follows has happened many times. Mary challenges in a more and more bitingly sarcastic manner. John says nothing, pretending to be absorbed in the newspaper. She climaxes her scene by running into the bedroom from where she can be heard sobbing. He responds by wadding up the newspaper, throwing it on the floor and then stomping out of the house, making sure the door slams loud enough to be heard by Mary. Early the next morning there is a reconciliation scene during which all talk about last night's bout is omitted so that the game can be put in storage just as it is, unaltered, ready for use whenever the occasion calls for it.

The beginning of the defensive game is an excellent time to begin a role reversal. John and Mary are seeing me for marital counseling. After Mary has responded sarcastically, I say, "I'd like you to change roles for a moment. Mary, change seats with John. You're John now. John, you're Mary."

It is very important that the participants actually exchange seats, both from the point of view of setting the scene for literally taking the other's place, and in order to avoid confusion when both go back to being themselves again. If John and Mary haven't reversed roles before, I may take a little time to set the scene. I will say to Mary, "Let's see, as John, tell me how you're feeling about things as you begin this talk with Mary. You've just had some good news, is that right?"

Mary (bitterly): That's right. I'm a big wheel at work.
Eva: What kind of big wheel are you, John?
Mary: Well, I get the most commissions in the place. I know how to sell. So I get higher pay and the bosses think I'm great. *(Mary laughs.)* It's really different at home!
Eva: Is there anything you want to tell Mary, over here, about that? What's different at home?

Mary: Well, Mary, you don't ever seem to think anything I do is right. (*Mary is still smiling self-consciously.*)

Eva: Go ahead, Mary, how about responding to that?

John: Well, all you care about is your work. That's all you care about. That's why you're gone all the time. I'm going to get a job as your secretary so I can see you every once in a while. (*John, too, is smiling as he does Mary's part of the familiar routine.*)

Mary (more serious): Well . . . you just blame me all the time. How can I show you anything? I get so mad at you!

John is visibly relieved as he sees Mary accurately describing the trap he falls into. At this point, there is a change which would help the original conversation. If John could actually comment on what he's feeling instead of counterattacking or withdrawing, the game could not continue in the same way. Mary, playing his role, has shown him how to comment on his feelings. He could say, "I get so mad at you," instead of hiding behind the newspaper. Consequently, I choose this time to ask John and Mary to change roles again. "O.K., how about changing chairs again and going back to being yourselves? John, could you start with the last sentence Mary said in your place: 'Well, if you blame me all the time, how can I show you anything? I get so mad at you!'" Technically, it is very helpful to give the participants the exact sentence with which to start the next scene. This maneuver insures that the scene will continue at the point which the leader deems crucial, and it also has the advantage of reducing the participants' confusion. Instead of thinking: *Let's see, now I'm back to being myself again, what did she just say to me? Should I start this? Or should I wait until she says something?* John simply says the sentence given to him by the leader.

The leader, of course, has the option of stopping after any role reversal and asking the participants to comment. "John, how did you feel about Mary's portrayal of you? Could you tell her what you liked and didn't like?" My own preference is to go through the scene, using role reversals where they seem most likely to help the couple shift into a more useful way of talking—and leave the talking about the role-playing for later. Talking *about* always lessens the dramatic flow. Only with a couple that shows a great deal of resistance and needs a lot of help from me in order to reverse roles at all, might I stop after the first reversal, with the hope that talking would provide encouragement for further work: "When you played me, you were really right on about my feeling hurt. How did you know I felt that way?" or "I don't think I talk like you did, I don't feel angry when that happens. I feel more hurt. . . ." In both instances, we can continue the work. The first comment may lead to an exploration of the ways in which Mary disguises her understanding of John's feelings: she's afraid to confront him directly, thinks he would be upset if he knew she knew, etc. Further scenes can be done to discover new ways in which Mary can talk to John more directly. In the second instance, John can show Mary how he sees himself acting in the same situation, and the group's comments can help analyze any discrepancies.

Of course, individuals new to role-reversal may also react negatively when we stop for comments. "I don't think I'm like that. You're just being mean. You don't understand me at all." If Mary feels this way, it is important for her to have a chance to say so; she certainly won't be able to cooperate fully in the role-playing while feeling like a victim. The leader can then attempt to clarify the communication between John and Mary. Was John "goading" Mary by his portrayal and adding a new twist to the old game? Or was he simply trying to show her something he perceived about her? When the issues are clarified and we are, once again, outside the territory of the "game," the role-playing can be resumed. Or, the leader may want to adopt a different strategy altogether and help Mary out of her dilemma by further role-playing:

Leader: Mary, you're saying that John didn't talk the way you do. Is that right?

Mary: Yes. I don't say things like 'I'm going home to mother.' He's just making fun of me. I haven't seen my mother in years.

Leader: What would you have said at this point in the conversation?

Mary: Well, I guess I'd say, 'I'm fed up to here. Really fed up.'

Leader: O.K., John, could you say that line?

John: I'm fed up to here.

Leader: Mary, is that more like you'd say it?

Mary: It is. That's what I'd say.

Leader: O.K., then maybe we can go back to the scene now. Mary, be John again and respond to what he just said.

With this strategy, we can circumvent the discussion about John's and Mary's conflict by attempting a solution which gives Mary some control in an area where she fears ridicule.

Role reversal is an excellent technique in any group organized with a hierarchy. In most of my work settings, there are staff members and patients. In some, there are students and teachers. Wherever there are such clearly drawn roles—parents and children, husbands and wives, visitors and inmates, employers and employees—it is often profitable to base one or several psychodrama sessions on role reversal. A warm-up on a psychiatric ward, for example, may involve my asking each person to choose a member of the other class about whom he has had some strong feelings: "If you are a patient, choose a staff member; if you are staff, choose someone who is a patient here." After giving the group some time in which to make a considered choice, I will ask each group member to act the part of the other person and to say one or two sentences in reference to himself. For example, John is a patient and picks Dr. K., about whom he has had some strong feelings. He is now to act the role of Dr. K. saying one or two sentences about John: "John just isn't getting anywhere. He just sits and won't talk," for example. I usually listen to each group member and then use a short feedback session to set up further scenes in which the staff–patient relationship is reversed. With parents and children, the group can be asked to pair off—one parent, one child—and explore a recent conflict. In institutions where there are ongoing relationships, it is often possible to take a recent issue which involves the whole community and explore it with role reversals. New rules about room inspection were explored with house matrons and inmates of a girls' home with much greater ease and considerable good humor once a role reversal had taken place, for example. In groups accustomed to using this technique, participants often ask for it: "I had a real set-to with Jane about coming here today, I'd like to try reversing roles and working on it."

If the leader is interested in working on parent–child conflicts, there is an excellent warm-up which explores some aspects of role reversal in a situation where there is physical disparity. The group is divided into couples. Each couple is asked to decide who will be parent, who will be child, how old the child is, and what the conflict to be worked on is. For example, a 5-year-old might be refusing to eat his meals, a 16-year-old might be challenging his father's rules about the use of the family car. One prop is necessary; each couple needs one chair.

The leader then asks the couples to begin role-playing their conflicts with the parent sitting on the chair and the child on the floor. After a few minutes, during which the leader has made sure that each couple has found an argument which can be prolonged for awhile, the leader asks the parent to stand up and continue the conflict. In this first series, the child remains sitting while the parent first sits on the chair, then stands up, then stands on the chair. The same roles and the same scene are continued throughout all of these changes. The second series of movements involves the parent's sitting on the floor while the child first sits on the chair, then stands up, then stands on the chair, still continuing the same conflict. While this is not a total role reversal, the exercise does permit both players to experience the conflict from the reverse vantage point. The last step of the exercise involves the couple's choosing a position where both are at the same level and concluding the argument.

This is a warm-up which is usually joined with a good deal of enthusiasm and which escalates in noise and excitement. (If the leader would prefer less confused presentation of this exercise, he could ask just one couple to demonstrate it for the whole group.) Group discussions following the exercise usually abound with feelings about the struggle for authority: "I couldn't give any orders, I just felt more and more helpless the higher I got." . . . "I really liked being on top. Being small was awful. It reminded me of when I was little." . . . "When the child was standing on the chair and I was on the floor, that was perfect. Just like I feel at home. Like the kids are giants." . . . "I liked being level. That's the best way to talk, no matter who you're talking to." If there is time and sustained group interest, the whole exercise can be repeated with reversed roles.

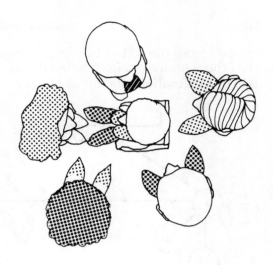

Chapter 6

The Sociogram

This technique, derived from the social sciences, is of immense use in acquainting the therapist with his terrain: the important relationships of an individual to his family, his job situation, his friends, whatever group has significance in his life. In sociology (I often begin my description of a sociogram this way when I am working with a group), a sociogram is a pictorial representation of an individual in relation to his group. We all remember having seen diagrams depicting John's popularity among his peers. John, represented by the circle with the J, has one close friend, Tommy, represented by the circle immediately next to his. He has three other friends, less close—children who live in his neighborhood whom he sees occasionally after school: Mary, Ted, and Jack. He feels fairly

isolated from the rest of his classmates and even more so from
the other children in his neighborhood. A graphic representation of his situation might look like this:

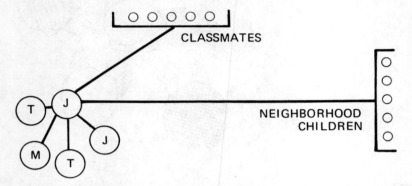

Anyone who sees this picture can form some hypotheses about
John's life. He may be a member of a minority group—social,
intellectual, or racial. His isolation may be based on some trait
which he shares with his friend Tommy. The hypotheses can
be varied and many.

The psychodramatic sociogram is a living picture. Instead of
being represented by a circle on a piece of paper, John actually
sits or stands in the center of his sociogram, assigning others in
the group to roles and positions fitting significant life relationships.

As the leader of the group, I may want to use the sociogram
to find out more about John's family relationships. If the
group is unfamiliar with the technique, I may begin by ex-
plaining something about the nature of the sociogram to the
whole group. I then ask John whether he is interested in exploring his family relationships with this technique. If he is
willing, my next step involves asking him to put his chair—or
himself, standing—in the center of the circle; I often go there
with him so that he does not experience an overdose of stage
fright. I then ask John to name those members of his family
most important to him, past and present. I usually add that he
may want to include someone who has died; if the person was

important in his life at one time, chances are that this significance was not erased by his death. As John names his family members, I ask him to find group members who could take the roles of these individuals. If John is taking the task seriously, it is often difficult for him to cast the group members: he can find no one who resembles his mother in any way, for example. If this occurs, the leader can give him support by validating the impossibility of anyone's really taking the place of his mother: "I know there isn't anyone here who has just those unique qualities that make your mother the person she is. What I want you to do is to choose someone who might be able to play the role, to approximate some part of her." It is important for the leader to avoid helping John choose by designating group members to play roles. John will choose individuals with qualities which have some emotional significance for him; no one else can know what these are. After John has assigned a role, I ask him to place the role-player in relationship to himself in space—as close or as far away as the relationship requires. I also ask him to show the role-player a posture which is typical. He may choose to place the person playing his mother standing over him, or sitting with her back turned in a resigned or dominant posture; any number of distances and positions can be found which typify a given relationship. Again, it is important that John chooses the distance and position of the role-players rather than passively accepting the way they choose to play themselves. After John has assigned a place and position in relation to himself to each of the significant family members he has chosen, the first part of the sociogram is complete. We can now see a living picture of John and his family.

The second part of the sociogram involves giving words and action to our living picture. My instructions to John begin with my asking him to think of one sentence for each person that is typical of the way that person might talk to him. John may make the task more difficult than it is. He may have a difficult time thinking of even a first sentence because he may understand the task to mean that he is to find *the* sentence which exemplifies the other person's attitude towards him. Therefore it is important to be clear in the instructions: "Think of a sentence you might hear from this person. Just any of the things he usually says when you get together." The leader accepts any sentence the protagonist offers. My own experience ranges from a simple "Hi" to "What is your reason for existence, my boy?" As leader, I know that the emotional involvement will emerge as we work further; all I need now is a start. As John gives each person his sentence, I ask the role-players to commit it to memory so that they can say it when the time comes. After John has given a sentence to each of the people in his sociogram, my instructions to the role-players are: "Now I want you each, in the order that John called you up here, to say your sentence to him. John won't answer you this time around, he'll just listen so that he can have some idea of how you are playing the role he assigned you." I usually help the role-players by nodding to them as their turn to speak comes up. After each person has said his sentence, I ask John, "How did they do? Look around the group once. Is there anyone whom you could help say the sentence more like the real person?" If John has some suggestions for changes in the role-playing ("My father would say that in a more aggressive tone," for example), I usually discourage further description of the differences and ask John to role-reverse with the person in order to show him how his father would say the line.

The third and final part of the sociogram involves John himself and allows him to interact with each member of his sociogram. My instructions to the role-players are, "I'm going to ask you each to say your sentence again, and this time I'm going to ask John to answer you. Then I want you to have a short conversation with John, continuing in your role. I know you don't know exactly what your character would say— there's no way you could—so I'm going to ask you to just follow your intuition, and continue talking with John until I stop you." Again, I usually give a signal that starts the dialogue with the person John called up first. As I observe the dialogue, I may want to help the participants reach a level of greater emotional significance. I can do this by using such strategies as doubling for the protagonist or giving a specific structure to the dialogue, such as asking John to focus on telling the other person exactly what he is feeling during this conversation, to focus on making demands on the other person, to focus on letting the other person know what he doesn't like about him, etc. Often, however, no interventions are needed. A short exchange between John and each family member provides all the information we need in order to form some hypotheses about the relationship:

Mother (saying sentence assigned by John): When did you get home last night?
John: About 10:30.
Mother: I was worried about you. I wished you had phoned to tell me when you'd be home.
John: I'm sorry.

Wife: Are they helping you at the Day Treatment Center?
John: I think the pills are making me worse.
Wife: I do too, why don't you stop taking them?
John: I probably should, but they tell me to take them.
Wife: Are you feeling any better?
John: No. I'm sorry.

Brother: You're going to be alright, John. Just stick to eating right and getting some exercise.
John: Thank you, George.
Brother: Have you tried going for some long walks; that always helps me when I'm nervous. Of course I never get as bad as you get.
John: I've tried it. Thanks for suggesting it.

In each dialogue, John plays a passive, receptive role. As we watch him, we wonder whether he doesn't have some angry feelings toward all those fine people who are watching him and trying to help him at every turn. We may want to explore this hypothesis by giving him a double who would make these feelings explicit. If John accepts our hypothesis and validates the double's sentiments ("It's true. I just wish they'd shut up and leave me alone some of the time. They seem to think I'm not trying"), our next step is clear. We can complete a part of the work with him by replaying the original scenes, this time with an effort on John's part to confront his negative feelings and make them explicit.

In any sociogram, after the dialogues have been completed, the leader and the other group members can choose those dialogues which they would like to see explored further.

The sociogram provides a simple structure for getting acquainted with a new group or new group members. Our timid clinician is given a tool which will help him bridge gaps by providing a clear, simple task, concrete enough for easy cooperation. The step-by-step directions offer frequent supportive contact with the leader. Group members usually enjoy being chosen to play roles in the protagonist's sociogram. The protagonist himself does not have to do a great deal of talking during the initial phases of the sociogram and is consequently able to participate at a more gradual pace than if he were to step into a scene which requires immediate full participation.

My work on psychiatric wards often leads to contact with individuals under severe stress who talk little about their outside lives. The sociogram not only offers an excellent means of gaining information about such individuals, but does so in a way that has a startlingly small potential for failure. An example is a sociogram with an adolescent boy, a foster child who was suspicious in his manner and sparse in his conversation. In assigning a sentence to each family member, he gave the same word to each person: "Hi." When I encouraged him to give a slightly more detailed version of something each person might say to him, he seemed not to understand and repeated that people just usually said "Hi" when they saw him. I had many doubts about the value of continuing with so little information, but I remembered that the boy was cooperating. He had chosen several people to play roles in his family, he was sitting in the center of the stage area. With a little patience perhaps something could be learned yet. Then, as he answered each person (needless to say, he answered by saying "Hi" as well), a staff member noticed a heightening of tension in his body as he answered his mother. Asked about this, he answered that he had read his mother's "Hi" as a cross-examination concerning his whereabouts and had stiffened defensively in response. With this information as a base, I encouraged the woman playing the role of the mother to continue in her role, and found our reticent adolescent increasingly vocal and informative.

The sociogram has been especially useful to me when doing a single consultation with a group which is new to me. After the warm-up, I ask one of the group members to do a sociogram of the group from his point of view. If the group is large, I may limit him to the 6 or 7 individuals most important to him. In a work situation, he may see certain members close, others far away; he may have a special place for the boss, etc. Often, after one sociogram is completed, other group members volunteer to do their own version and, as the initial work is done, a map of the crucial relationships in the group emerges more and more clearly.

The uses of the sociogram are, of course, many and varied. A family therapist may want to ask an individual to do a sociogram using his actual family members; a group therapist may wish to ask an individual to graph his social relationships in the group; the sociogram may include dwellers in the same apartment house, friends, neighbors, shopkeepers—the sky's the limit. The technique's only requirement is time: I would not begin a sociogram unless I knew that I had 30 to 45 minutes to work it through.

Chapter 7

The Empty Chair

This technique was developed by Fritz Perls, the founder of Gestalt therapy, as a major tool for dramatizing and working out internal conflicts. It is immensely useful to any therapist using role-playing techniques. My own acquaintance with the empty chair stems from my personal encounter with Perls, the technique, and the thunder of my own internal conflicts; the experience taught me a great deal about myself and provided a bonus in the form of this new technique and some of its specific applications.

Where others use role-playing, Perls uses an empty chair. If a person, for example, wants to work on a problem involving his mother-in-law, Perls' response would be: "Put your mother-in-law in the empty chair and then talk to her." John, who had chosen to work on his problem, would have indicated his choice by walking over to the "hot seat," the seat next to Perls himself, opposite which the proverbial empty chair was located. In my own work, I prefer to move over to the person who wishes to work, rather than using the "hot seat," and will usually ask to change seats with whomever is sitting beside John and then ask someone to provide us with an extra chair, to be placed directly opposite him. I have found it important to sit close to the working individual, both in order to give him the support of my own nearness so that I can show him that I am really listening and touch him reassuringly, if necessary, and also so that I can be in the best possible position to listen and to observe nonverbal clues.

If John seems to have some difficulty initially because of the unfamiliarity of the task, I may—following Perls' example as I will be in the rest of this section—tell him to begin by saying: "Before you talk to her, why don't you tell us who you see there. Visualize her sitting on that chair. Tell us what you see."

It is most useful to coach John so that he gives us concrete physical details, helping him to visualize the actual, physical person. "Well, let's see, she's about 5′ 5″, sort of dumpy, about sixty years old. One thing, her mouth is always going. She never stops yakking. Yak, yak, yak."

In the latter part of his description, John has supplied us with the beginning of his dialogue; here is something he is upset with, something he could be saying to his mother-in-law to help him start to develop the conflict. It is important to listen for any such emotionally charged phrases; they provide the natural bridge to the dialogue.

John cooperates and now addresses the empty chair: "Jeez, Mom, you just never shut up. Your mouth is always going. You never stop yakking. Yak, yak, yak" (turning to me) "but I'd never tell her that." I may make it clear to John at this point that we are interested in getting at his inner conflicts, that this is not a rehearsal to be repeated in real life, unless he chooses to do so.

We will then continue with my saying to John, "Well, you just said it. Let's see how she reacts. Switch chairs. Be your mother-in-law and react to what John just said." It is important that John actually switches chairs before continuing—just as it is in any role reversal—to help him concretize his task and avoid the confusion that often results when several roles are played in the same location. John, playing his mother-in-law, now says, "Oh, I have never been so hurt! I don't believe it! After all I've done for you kids." From here on in, the therapist's task is to help John develop the dialogue in a way which will help him express feelings which he holds back in real life.

The dialogue may help John understand something about the meaning of his conflict as well. For example, the therapist may notice that John, instead of becoming angrier and angrier, seems to lose vocal power, to become more and more the little boy as he addresses his mother-in-law.

"You're always right, aren't you," John whines, "you make me sick. You don't even know what you're talking about."

The therapist can then ask John, "How old do you feel?" If John acknowledges feeling like a boy, the next question is "As a boy, who would you be talking to like that? Who would you say that to" (choosing the last phrase heard in the dialogue) "'You make me sick. You don't even know what you're talking about.'" When John makes the connection to a more primary character in the drama of his own life, "It's true, that's just like my grandma that used to live with us and I'm acting like I did when I was seven," the empty chair now becomes that person—Grandma, in John's case—enabling him to continue working at a deeper level.

The empty chair is invaluable to the therapist who is seeing an individual. He can now use role-playing in the individual's therapy hour as well as in a group. Even in a group, the empty chair may have advantages: unlike role-playing group members, it is always informed about the real situation, sensitive to the working individual, dependable for continued work, etc. The empty chair can be used as a way to introduce group

members to new characters in an individual's drama; the
therapist may ask group members whether anyone feels he
could now play the role of, for example, John's mother-in-law,
after observing several exchanges with John playing the role in
the empty chair. The empty chair provides direct experience
in a most economical and simple manner. Perls developed it as
a way to avoid the deadening intellectualization of "talking
about" problems and conflicts.

So far, we have discussed the aspects of the empty chair
technique which correlate closely with conventional role-
playing. The technique can also be used in a very special way,
to act out symbols, metaphors, and dreams which help the individual get in touch with those aspects of inner conflicts
which are not necessarily interpersonal, but which represent
inner struggles, fears, anxieties.

For example, here is a part of my own work with Perls. I
had occupied the empty chair at great emotional expense.
Even after some initial work I was mainly conscious of my
fear.

Perls: Can you close your eyes and visualize your fear? Give
it a landscape. Stay with your feeling of fear. What do you
see?

Eva (surprised that the images flow so readily): I see an attic. Just a part of the attic with a brown wood floor. I can see
the texture of the wide boards. It's dark and cold and at the
very back of the attic, way back, there's a blue light.

Perls: Could you talk for the floor boards. Be the floor.
What does it say?

Eva: I'm brown, and old, very worn. I'm dark. I'm cold.
I'm really alone. No one ever comes here. (*I start to cry, experiencing a desolate loneliness.*) There are no people here at
all.

Perls: Now go over to the empty chair and be the blue light.

Eva (changing chairs): I'm way back of the attic. I'm light.
I'm cold, too. I'm very beautiful, an icy blue. I can see my rays
a short way through the window along the floor.

Perls: What do you have to say to the floor boards?

Eva: You're so dark and ugly. Why don't you come into the light?

Perls: Switch chairs and answer.

Eva (switching chairs): Because I can't move. (*Again, I am conscious of great pain.*) I can't touch you. You have to come to me. (*I don't feel at all hopeful that this will happen.*)

Perls: Switch again.

Eva: I can't do anything about your feelings. I am where I am. You have to come to me.

Perls: Switch again. Now ask the light, "How can I touch you without being frozen out?"

As I hear Perls ask the question, I become conscious that he is addressing a part of myself that has done a great deal of "freezing out"—refusing the warmth of others in a haughty, cold manner. The work has put me in touch with my loneliness and also with the part of me that insures that no inroads are made on it. Perls has me say, "I can freeze you out" to several group members. I do it with conviction. My mood lightens. I tell Perls that I feel better. He asks me to shut my eyes again and to visualize my present mood.

Eva: Now I feel as though it's a warm day. I really feel warm. I feel like I'm just slightly underwater in a lake. And I can feel some seaweeds just lightly brushing up against me.

Perls: Can you do that to some of the people in the group? Just lightly brush up against them?

I do. I lightly touch one person's hand, another's face, another's shoulder. I feel relieved. There's also a part of me that can connect with others. I feel that I want to be warmer. Maybe I can leave some of that coldness with the past, when I needed the self-protection it offered.

The empty chair can act out inanimate objects, dream figures, metaphors—roles which would be nearly impossible to cast with real persons because their inner significance is known only to their creator.

Perls believes that every aspect of our metaphor or dream is a projection. The dream that I am a grasshopper being devoured by a cat contains not only the fear of being toyed with, being eaten alive, but also my sadistic element, my devourer, the part of me that toys with others. The dialogue between the grasshopper and the cat puts me in touch with my weak–strong polarity, an inner conflict which I need to resolve. A dream involving an empty parking lot being filled with cars produced a dialogue in which the dreamer got in touch with his passive, blank way of resisting (the parking lot) both internal and external active moving forces (the cars).

A metaphor may be observed in an individual's posture. If I notice an individual's hand gesture, I may say, for example, "Could you take a look at what your hands are doing?" I may have to caution the individual not to change the position of his hands, just to observe them. The right hand is clenched. The left hand is covering it, the thumb making stroking gestures. Right and left hands now have a dialogue which shows us the individual's tension and anxiety, maybe even anger, on the one hand (literally) and his neediness, his want of comfort, love, and affection, on the other. A simple way of eliciting a meaningful metaphor—this last phrase is almost redundant, as I am hard put to imagine a meaningless metaphor—if the individual does not remember dreams, or evidence much in the way of nonverbal gestures, is to do what Perls did with me in my work: to ask the individual to close his eyes and visualize a given mood. Whenever someone is experiencing an emotion— fear, withdrawal, laughter, frustration, anger—this strategy involves asking the individual to "Visualize this mood. Close your eyes and see if you can go into your feeling. Give it a landscape. Give us pictorial details of the landscape your feeling calls up."

There is one other use of the empty chair which may prove quite dramatic. When, during a family interview, or during a psychodrama of a given scene, a character who is no longer alive or who is absent from the scene in some other way seems to take on a great deal of emotional importance, an empty chair can be used to represent that person. Now the others in the scene are no longer able to talk *about* the individual; they are directed to talk *to* him, as though he were once more among them. The strategy may involve having some member of the scene play the part of the absent member some of the time, or it may not. I am inclined to leave the chair empty throughout the scene—a symbol of the absent member, dead parent, divorced father, etc. Often the remarks addressed to the empty chair are really messages for someone present, messages that have been diverted because of the convenient scapegoating of the absent member. This strategy also often allows us to take up unfinished grief situations—situations in which death or departure came suddenly, or in which the remaining members inhibited their feelings—by allowing the expression of sorrow, anger, or love hitherto suppressed.

Anyone interested in pursuing the use of these techniques further must read the Perls books. One does not have to be a Gestalt therapist to use the technique of the empty chair. It is a bridge to the investigation of the metaphor, to direct emotional experience, for any therapist that uses the active techniques.

Chapter 8

Six Characters in Search of a Personality

The six-character technique is taught by Virginia Satir, who has made many innovative contributions to the experiential therapies, especially to family therapy. Although there are many techniques which help us dramatize a given individual's relationships to others, fewer exist for the purpose of exploring the inner life of the individual. The six-character technique provides such a dramatic structure.

The six-character technique has a special quality that demands patients who are both verbal and imaginative and a group that can proceed at a leisurely pace. It will not work in a crisis. This exercise takes us on an excursion into the soul of the individual who is working.

The directions are as follows: "I want you to think of six well-known characters, six famous creations—three men and three women. They can be from any age and any medium: book, play, movie, fairy tale, etc. They should be three men and three women who have meant something to you as you grew up or in your adult life."

The more literate and/or imaginatively spontaneous the individual, the more easily he responds to the task. Individuals who have difficulty thinking of famous names often ask whether real people may be included. I let them be included only as a last resort as I see great value in the evocation of archetypes called forth by associations to fame and legend.

After the individual has selected the six characters, he is asked to choose a group member to play each role. In order to help those playing the roles to grasp the protagonist's version of their existence, I further ask him to supply each role player with three adjectives which describe his character. For example, one protagonist chose Captain Ahab and the Sphinx among his six characters. For Ahab, he gave the following three adjectives: "Restless, driven, obsessed." For the Sphinx, he said: "Wise, elliptical, catlike." (I will describe his scene in detail later.)

After all six characters have been selected, the directions continue: "Now we are going to invite all six of your characters to a party where they will meet and talk with one another. You will stay on the sidelines with me and watch." The leader then designates the stage area and directs each character to say his name as he joins the party. Usually, some awkwardness accompanies the beginning of the scene, as the role-players begin to work into their roles. As the scene progresses, it often happens that the group is divided by antagonisms and coalitions which vividly represent our protagonist's inner conflicts. The leader's job is to remain sensitive to the protagonist so that he can help him cope with the scene he has evoked. After ten minutes or so, the leader asks the protagonist to help the role-players by suggesting changes he deems necessary. If the scene becomes chaotic, or if an argument in the scene reaches an impasse, the leader directs the protagonist to suggest ways of resolving the difficulty to the characters in the scene.

The length of the scene is up to the leader's discretion. In my own experience, the actual "party" usually lasts 15–20 minutes. At a time when I feel that most of the conflicts and polarities potential in the scene have been explored, I usually stop the scene and ask the protagonist what he experienced as he watched. Typically, he begins by answering, "That's exactly what it's like for me all the time. That's me. That's the way I talk inside myself." I may then explore further with him what he learned about himself as he saw the scene.

There are several strategies which enable the leader to explore the scene psychodramatically even further. He may ask each of the players to give a monologue in which he describes his feelings while he played his character. The leader may ask the protagonist to do two things: (1) to say to each character in turn "You are my . . . (tenderness, hatred, energy, etc.)," and (2) to arrange his six characters in a sculpture which shows their relationship to each other (the humble Siddhartha may be on the bottom of a pyramid topped by the greedy Miser, for example) and then to fit himself into the sculpture in the end.

The six-character technique suggests many topics for further exploration in the group. Does the individual like what he sees? Now that he has had a look at the party, are there any characters he wants to explore? The protagonist can pose questions, set up specific conflicts, impose monologues which let him know secret thoughts—in short, he can direct his characters to do whatever he wants. After he has seen his characters in action, he may want to explore his reactions with a double who could help him integrate the experience.

An Example

Soon after I had learned the six-character technique from Virginia Satir, I became an enthusiastic proponent. The following is an example of its use in an individual's group composed of young unmarried people who had been meeting together for two hours a week for about a year. Several people had tried out the technique during the several weeks preceding

Michael's work. The group had responded enthusiastically to the opportunity of acting roles which had such universal appeal. It was a group in which a standing joke was that no one—including the therapist—could give up being "special," no matter what the cost. It was easier to find someone right for the part of Jesus Christ than for the role of a group member's father who ran a grocery store in the Bronx.

Soon after the group began, Michael volunteered, asking to use the six-character technique. He had been giving it a good deal of thought, he said, and already had his characters in mind. Michael is a man in his early thirties, an architect known for his originality and his moodiness. The other group members responded positively to his request. He frequently wore an arrogant, aloof expression that made it difficult to approach him. Perhaps this would be a chance to get to know him better.

I asked Michael to cast his six characters from group members . . . to chat with each of them in order to find out how each saw the role he was assigned to play. I also asked him to fill them in on what he wanted in each character. Further, I asked Michael to give each person three adjectives that would describe the qualities of action he wanted.

Michael chose three men first. He asked the oldest member of the group, Robert, a highly gifted mathematician, to play Captain Ahab from Melville's *Moby Dick*, giving him the adjectives "restless, driven, obsessed." Robert knew and loved *Moby Dick* as well; there seemed to be an immediate understanding about what Michael wanted in the part.

Next, Michael asked Tad to play Siddhartha. Tad was a bit of a bohemian, a quiet young man with soulful eyes. He was not familiar with the Hesse book from which the character derived, but he had read a great deal about the Buddha in books dealing with Zen Buddhism and seemed to grasp easily what Michael wanted. His adjectives were "kind, quiet, responsive."

The next characters Michael selected were Pagliacci, from the opera about the sad, cuckolded clown, and Rima, the woodland sprite from Hudson's *Green Mansions*. Leah, playing Rima, was unfamiliar with Hudson's novel, but so right for the part that everyone knew she would have no difficulty. Michael selected June to play Ayn Rand—type-casting, they said in the group, for June was a powerful individual of considerable intensity in her manner. Her adjectives were similar to Ahab's "restless, powerful, intense." Last, he asked Justine to play the Sphinx; her adjectives were, "catlike, elliptical, wise."

The characters entered in the order of their selection. First, Captain Ahab. He looked gaunt, his facial expression even more tense and inward than usual. He introduced himself as he had been asked to do: "Captain Ahab." He gave a few short glances to his surroundings, apparently judged them lacking in attraction, and found a place near a window. During the rest of the scene, he looked out the window, making only short sorties into the conversation taking place at the party.

The Sphinx entered. She was a tall, wise-looking woman who conveyed a feline air by her movement. She looked about, a Mona Lisa smile on her face as she encountered Ahab's glance. "I am the Sphinx," she purred. (The group reacted with some surprise; Justine had not shown herself so seductive before.)

Rima bounced in. She was young and pretty, dark ringlets cascading about her face. She had taken her shoes off. Her face was quiet and relaxed, yet she seemed to be smiling. She walked directly up to the Sphinx. "Hello, I'm Rima, a friend of Michael's. I've never seen you before. Do you know him well?" The Sphinx, who had made herself comfortable on a nearby sofa, said nothing for a while, apparently appraising Rima, who seemed to enjoy being looked over. Then the Sphinx said, "I know him better than he wishes me to."

As she was speaking, Tad entered, introducing himself as "Siddhartha." It was immediately apparent that he meant to talk to Rima. They were quickly involved in a conversation about the surrounding forest. The Sphinx looked on quietly; bemused, interested.

Ayn Rand came in. An older woman like the Sphinx, but her opposite in character. Restless, apparently aggressive, but without a target. She took to her part with obvious relish. (In the group, people often told June to slow down. Now she could be as quick and intense as she liked.) Ayn Rand paced the room. She thought that perhaps she and the Sphinx had met before at a writer's conference. When the Sphinx smiled "no," she attempted a conversation with Ahab, who also put her off, making it clear that he wished no connection with her of any kind. Ayn seemed surprised for a moment. It was difficult for her to believe that she was not the center of attention. She began to pace again, obviously hoping to break into the intense conversation between Rima and Siddhartha.

Pagliacci entered. He was appealing in his hippie attire, a sad look in his eye, apparently searching the room for someone who might understand him or show him some warmth. He introduced himself, then walked over to the Sphinx's sofa and sat cross-legged on the floor in front of it.

"I remember you," she said, "the last time I saw you I had to avoid you because I knew something you didn't know."

"I guess everybody knew but me," he countered sadly. "Maybe it was better that way."

"Surely," said the Sphinx. "But that was a few months ago. You're not still sad over that woman?"

"No," said Pagliacci sadly, "I'm much happier now."

The Sphinx looked around the room. "Happiness is like water," she said, "crystal clear in one moment and opaque the next."

On the other side of the stage area, Ayn Rand, addressing Siddhartha, said, "I really have no taste for these things; they seem so artificial to me. What do you think?" He had looked at her with some surprise because she had interrupted the silence he and Rima were enjoying. Now he turned to her, but before he could answer, she continued in a hasty, intense way, spewing out words in a torrent, "I *know* I've met you before. I said that to the lady over there and it didn't turn out to be true, although it still could be true as far as I'm concerned. People don't always remember. *I* usually do. But you, you. . . . Where did we meet? You look a great deal like a young man who used to work for me as a sort of secretary, but of course that wasn't you. Could you be related? His name was Gau-tama." (June was making an intellectual point here—ob-viously enjoying the response she elicited from some of the others who had caught the reference.) "An Indian fellow, so, of course, you wouldn't be. But here is something so similar in quality. Something quiet about you, also, just waiting to be touched. I think I could help you find your creative energy. I think I could help you write. I have strong intuitions. . . ."

Siddhartha turned to see where Rima had gone. She had gone to another window, at the opposite side of the room. He touched Ayn Rand's hand and looked at her quietly. "I don't know what you want," he said, "maybe I was related to that other person but he and I aren't the same. Excuse me, there is a man here I would like to meet." And he began to walk to-ward Ahab.

An awkward period ensued. The scene began to take on the appearance of a real party that was going badly. People didn't seem to know what they were there for. Some looked to the therapist for help now and then but got only a quiet signal to continue. They milled about, saying a tentative word here and there but making no real connections. On the outside of the circle, Michael was visibly disturbed by what he saw. He looked at me with a frustrated expression. I asked him what he was feeling.

"Like it isn't really happening," he said. "All these strong characters and yet none seems right for the others. They each seem to be in their own world."

I asked Michael what he would like to have happen between the characters. Michael responded that he would like them to make a stronger effort to relate to each other. I asked him to speak to his six characters, asking them to become more in-volved, less self-centered.

"Where have I heard that before," he said, looking back at the rest of the group, smiling in recognition of a message he had heard many times in his life.

On stage, the characters were eyeing each other. Ayn Rand, catching a glimpse of Rima who was crossing the room, said, "This party isn't going anywhere. Come talk to me. You are a very pretty girl. Pretty girls usually love parties like this. But you don't look like you are enjoying yourself at all. Why not?"

"I'm afraid of that man," Rima answered, indicating Ahab. "He frightens me. He's like a dark force. I want to be light and happy but I can't as long as he's around."

She looked at the Sphinx who had been sitting on the sofa nearby, "What do you think?"

The Sphinx smiled at Pagliacci, who was still sitting near her. "Why do we have to have fun? Joy and truth are seldom united. Maybe yes. Maybe no. But I don't care. Anything is alright with me."

"You have a poetic quality," said Ayn Rand to the Sphinx, looking deeply into her eyes. "You are a very unusual person. You have power. I'm interested in power. Are you sure we haven't met before?"

The Sphinx turned towards her. "I'm sure," she said.

Ayn Rand's eyes began to scan the room restlessly once more.

Offstage, Michael asked me if he could stop the scene in order to arrange a dialogue between Siddhartha and Ahab. I encouraged him to do so.

Ahab was standing at the same window he had chosen when he came in. His expression was somber, uninviting.

Siddhartha approached him. He asked, "Would you mind talking to me a little? I've been looking at you. Are you angry about something?"

Ahab turned to look at Siddhartha. He looked angry. He seemed to consider not answering the young man and then to think better of it. "I am angry," he said, "that all these people are twiddling their lives away." Siddhartha asked him what he meant. "There's nothing going on in any of their souls," Ahab answered, "They're like mush. No substance. No character. I am a very different person. I can't be expected to get along with the likes of you."

Siddhartha looked concerned. "But you *are* different," he said. "You look like a man who is driven by a great cause. What is it?"

When Ahab described his obsession with the white whale, the sense of darkness that Rima had mentioned earlier became real for all the observers. His face twitched as he spoke. At times one had the feeling one could see sparks flying from his person, he was so intense. Everything else had been obliterated in his life so that only Moby Dick existed. Clearly there was no room for human concerns in this fanatic's life. (The role suited Robert, often accused of an exclusive attachment to his mathematics by others in his life.) And yet there was something attractive about his passion and his certainty. He *knew*. As we listened to him, we all became aware that Michael, the protagonist, could be similarly uncompromising.

Siddhartha had listened quietly, looking on Ahab with patience and kindness. "I know you know I am not like you," he said when Ahab came to a stop. "And I know that you wouldn't listen to me if I asked you to think more of the others in your life, to consider human values. You are on a mission and you must live through it. It's too bad. I wish you could have seen me." He looked a little sad as he said the last words.

I had noticed Michael's growing involvement and had stepped close to him, attempting to give him support by my presence. Michael had tears in his eyes as the dialogue ended. He looked at me. "It's like me and my father," he said, "only I'm the intense one and he is kind and forgiving. But we never seem to be able to get together."

I asked Michael if there was anything further he wanted his characters to do. Michael thought it over and said, "No, I don't think so. I'm still a little shaken by that Ahab part of me. I think I'd like a little time to take it in."

I asked the group to take a 5-minute breather. When we reconvened, I said to Michael, "I'd like you to do one other thing with your six characters. Tell each of them what quality of yours he represents. How would you feel about doing that now?"

Michael agreed and proceeded without difficulty. Naming these qualities seemed to help him finish, to settle something for himself.

To Ahab, he said: "You are my ruthlessness."

To Siddhartha: "You are my kindness."

To Pagliacci: "Oh, I'd forgotten all about you. You are my pathos."

To the Sphinx: "You are my wisdom."

To Rima: "You are my ideal."

To Ayn Rand: "You are my ruthlessness also. And my ambition."

Michael sighed deeply when he finished. He had been completely absorbed by the task. When we talked with him about what it had been like, afterwards, he seemed astounded that he could have obtained a dramatic version of his inner life. "There were so many familiar themes," he said, "but Ahab, he's the one that really got to me. What am I going to do with that part of me?"

I was pleased with the way the scene had gone. Michael's comment was correct. There were many themes we could return to: the polarity between the driving, obsessive demon and the love-starved young man, for example. When we reviewed the scene, Tom, who had played Pagliacci, commented that he had felt left out; everyone else had gotten more attention.

Another group member laughed, "Isn't that the story of your life, Michael, feeling left out?"

Michael joined in the laughter. "It's true. If I just didn't have to make such a federal case out of every little rejection."

I observed that Michael was relating easily to the others in the group. The scene had provided a much-needed bridge between him and the others.

Because the six-character technique requires a group with a number of individuals who are verbal, imaginative, playful, and introspective, I have not used it on the psychiatric ward, as I fear that it would provide too great a challenge to a group with a majority of members under severe stress. In groups where there is a growth-oriented atmosphere—encounter groups, therapy groups—the six-character technique has provided a stimulus for further spontaneity and use of the imagination. Eleanor Roosevelt, Elizabeth Taylor, Rima of *Green Mansions*, Lulu, Alice in Wonderland, the Sphinx, Little Red Riding Hood, Marlene Dietrich, Ahab, Moses, Ulysses, Hiawatha, Linus of "Peanuts," Siddhartha, The White Knight, St. Francis of Assisi, Little Lord Fauntleroy— the cast of possible characters is endless and the potential for group enrichment immense.

Chapter 9

The Given Scene

Each setting in which he or she works provides the psycho-drama leader with a number of scenes which are givens for the particular group environment in that they have some relevance for everyone there. At a meeting of the Parent-Teacher Association, these scenes will center around issues concerning parents, teachers, children, and issues relating to school, for example. A given scene for a PTA meeting might be one in which a parent is attempting to influence a teacher in regard to a grade given to his child, or a scene in which the parent or teacher is confronted by the child who refuses to obey, saying, "But my mother (teacher) lets me do it at home (school)." These scenes, which refer to issues common to all of the group members, are sometimes referred to as sociodrama. They provide work for the group in sessions in which the group and the leader are new to each other, or when there is a dearth of specific issues brought up by group members, or in sessions which the leader wishes to use to help pull his group together.

In order to find a given scene for a specific group, I ask myself the following questions: Who belongs to this group? Does the group have subgroupings which show potential conflicts (parents–children, parents–teachers, nurses–patients, etc.)? Does the purpose of the group give me a clue about potential problem areas (Alcoholics Anonymous, psychiatric ward, therapy group, probation officer training group)? What kind of warm-up would help me find the given scenes?

If I am new to the group, I try to use a warm-up which leads me into the given scene. At the PTA meeting, I may ask the group to divide into pairs and assign one member of each pair to the parent role and the other to the teacher role. If I have already thought of a useful scene, I may ask each couple to work on it. For example: "Now that you have assigned roles, I want the parents to be coming in to talk to the teacher about the *F* Johnny got in math. You parents are upset about the *F*; you feel it might ruin Johnny's chances for getting into the college of his choice. That is the only information I am giving you. The rest is up to you. Take a few minutes to decide how you wish to play the scene. Is Johnny bright or dull? Does the teacher wish to teach Johnny a lesson for being lazy? Are the parents overly ambitious? After you have decided, start your dialogues and continue until I tell you to stop. I will be coming around to listen to you." As I listen to the dialogues, it is easy to pick up issues common to more than one scene which can be used for further work for the whole group.

On the psychiatric ward where I work, there are several given scenes: the scene of the patient arriving at the hospital and talking to the admitting nurse; the scene of the patient returning home from the hospital; the scene in which the patient asks the therapist whether he is ready to leave; the scene in which the patient tries to find a new job after leaving the hospital. In the next section, I will describe the course of such a given scene—the job interview—during one session on a psychiatric ward.

The Job Interview

When I arrive to do my psychodrama group on the psychiatric ward of one of our large city hospitals, I learn that the patients discussed job interviews at the community meeting earlier in the day. Several unresolvable questions arose: Should you let a potential employer know about your hospitalization? Should you lie about it? If not, how could you talk about having been mentally ill?

I know the group to be especially lively, verbal, and intelligent from previous meetings. When my group begins, I decide to forego a warm-up and move right into a scene. "I hear you've been discussing the job scene. (*General assent.*) I'd like to do some more work on that if it's O.K. with you. Who is about to go out on a job interview?"

Shirley is a woman in her mid-thirties. She is nice-looking, neatly dressed, alert, energetic. Her body is held erect, tight with physical tension. She volunteers that she will be going to interviews with several employment counselors that afternoon. The sing-song of her voice betrays her former profession: elementary school teacher. Another patient volunteers to do the interviewing. In the opening scene, Shirley does very well. She states what she wants clearly—a job as a receptionist-typist—and looks out for her own interests in terms of time and money. She gives the impression of self-assured competence. Her hospitalization is not mentioned.

I get the feeling that both Shirley and the patient playing the interviewer are cooperating to stay away from threatening issues. I ask, "Is there a question you're afraid the interviewer may ask, Shirley?"

She answers, "Yes. It's because I've only had this one other business experience, the job with the undertaker. Other than that I was a teacher and I don't want to go into that, because then he'll ask why I'm changing and all that. Anyway, I don't even want to mention the job with the undertaker because they might ask for a reference."

"And?"

"And my old boss knows I came here. . . . Well, I quit working for him in a rather immature way. That is, really, I never quit. I came to the hospital and then I phoned him and told him I was here and I wouldn't be back."

Marilyn, an aggressive-looking younger woman who, on the surface, looks a great deal tougher than Shirley, nods her head, "I did the same thing." Several others comment that nothing is harder than to tell someone you're quitting.

I use this information about a common theme to set up further scenes. First, I ask Shirley, our undertaker's secretary, to phone up her former employer to discuss her references. We play the scene with two outcomes. In the first, the employer is happy to help Shirley out by omitting her hospitalization from his references. Shirley thanks him but lets us know that she doesn't think it would work this way; in reality the scene would be different. The second time, Shirley coaches her employer in the role: he would feel morally obligated to let others know that she has some mental problems; he would have to speak the truth, if asked. Again, Shirley astounds us with her firm, clear way of stating her wants. When she hears the bad news, she simply says, "Thank you, then I won't list you as a reference," and hangs up the phone. She is pleased with herself and tells us how different she feels from her earlier self, the woman who could not face quitting her job.

My own thoughts are that all this is just a little too easy. Shirley comes off competent, all right—but the scene provides for so little exchange of feeling that we can't judge anything about how easily her smooth surface might be ruffled. I ask her to do one other scene, the scene she avoided by coming to the hospital, the scene in which she confronts her boss and tells him she is quitting.

Now Shirley shows her other self. Before the scene begins, she wants to go on and on telling us why she needed to quit the job: the pay was terrible, she had to get up at 5:00 in the morning for the commute, she had been promised a raise, he was impossible to talk with, etc., etc. When she confronts him in the scene, she confesses her own inability to take pressure and whines that her children need her when they come home from school. It's as though she expects him to feel sorry for her and fire her for her own good.

The group dubs her "the Mouse," and she gets all kinds of advice on how to stand up for herself. Marilyn, the younger woman who seemed to identify with Shirley's problems earlier, shows Shirley how to be strong and tough in opposing her boss.

Of course, I know that Shirley can't copy Marilyn. She would be pretending a toughness that is not her own. I take what might appear to be a step backward and ask Shirley to act out her real feelings toward her boss, tough or not tough, whatever they are.

She says, "I don't know why I'm here. I know I'm wrong to quit. You've been nice just to put up with me. I know I'm just lucky to even have this job." She breaks up, laughing, "this crummy, dirty, cheap job, you bastard! O.K., look, you know it's a crummy job so I guess you can expect some turnover. I'm leaving at the end of the week." Shirley laughs again as she talks with the group, more in touch with a polarity inside her: the doormat versus the strong, free spirit.

Throughout Shirley's work, I have been conscious of some discrepant messages from Marilyn. She has been acting as though she knew what to do in this position, suggesting all kinds of threats through pressure from unions and government agencies for Shirley's funeral director boss, yet I remember that Marilyn had stated that she also had been unable to quit her job. When I ask her about that, she agrees that she feels much the way Shirley does. Marilyn wants to work on it. I ask her to play her boss, discussing Marilyn as a worker:

"She was really good. The best I ever had here. Dependable. Efficient. But then this crazy stuff. I just don't understand that at all."

What does he know about it, I ask.

"Nothing! Just one day she doesn't show up and then I get this letter a week later. She says she wants to come back, just for an hour or two to start with, and at first I thought it would be O.K., but now I don't know."

I ask Marilyn to choose someone else in the room to play her boss in order to do a scene in which she talks to him about returning to work. She behaves in a startlingly obsequious manner: "I liked working for you so much. . . . I always knew where I stood with you and no other boss was ever like that. . . . Even if I can't start again right away and you should hire someone else, if there is ever a time after that where you do need someone, would you give me a call?"

The group members are agreed that Marilyn is giving some double messages. Several people point out to Marilyn that she seems to be begging her boss to take her back, that she is saying: "Poor me, hire me because you pity me." Someone in the group guesses that, unlike Shirley, Marilyn doesn't want to work at all—that, actually, she is talking herself out of a job rather than into one. One theme pervades this session: "I can't decide whether I want work or pity more."

This is a bright, sensitive group, and the members quickly find out that Marilyn is deeply disappointed in her husband, who has been at home for the past three months since he was released from prison.

One of the ex-convicts in the group plays Marilyn's husband, smoothly conning, "You know I've tried to get work, but who's going to hire an ex-con? . . . So I get up late, so would you if you'd had prison hours for a year. . . . If I didn't care for you and the kids, would I be here?"

Marilyn makes abortive attempts to show her husband the firm toughness she had voiced earlier in group, but demonstrates over and over again that she is unable to take a firm stand. Coming to the hospital has been her only way of saying she doesn't want to take care of her husband anymore.

The group members point out to Marilyn that she presents a tough, aggressive front to the outside world which makes it difficult to see her soft, helpless side. It is easy to see that others rely on her for help without thinking that she needs some herself. She feels some support from the group, whose members, the day before, had described her behavior as hostile and distancing.

Here are two examples of work around the job interview. In the first, we stick to the actual job situation, using the scene to finish some unfinished business by investigating alternative solutions. The work with Shirley could have led to work with others who also wanted some practice in the job interview or to working on an alternative to her desired solution; namely, a scene in which someone who does wish to discuss the fact that he has been hospitalized (or has been mentally ill, or in psychiatric treatment, etc.) does so and examines the consequences. The work in our group led to an alternative frequent in psychotic groups—the examination of Marilyn's double message about work. Her words say "I want to work," but the tenor of the message is "Don't hire me." We could then do further work with the group on the more general issues relating to the sentiment that one has to appear strong while feeling very weak.

Almost everyone in an all-day or overnight treatment setting has some concerns about his ability to rejoin the outside world. The job interview provides one of the settings for examining these themes.

Chapter 10

The Magic Shop

Some techniques can be used as a warm-up, to fill up an hour, or to provide a whole day's work. The magic shop is one of these. It is a very special technique which, at its best, recalls the wisdom and spontaneity of fairy tales and children.

When I give the directions, I usually assume a tinge of the storyteller. My object is to weave a slight spell—I have to say slight; what if I baldly admitted I wanted to weave a spell and couldn't?—to create an atmosphere of play, magic, daring, to establish metaphor as king, to encourage extravagant projection. I may use this technique because it's raining out and I need cheering up, or because everyone in the group seems to want to be someone else. Whatever the reason, when the magic shop takes hold, it usually takes the rest of the session, however long. When it doesn't take hold, it's like any magic that fizzles out—disappointing, tawdry, boring, and somehow infuriating. This is a far-out technique most useful for far-out people. I don't usually try it with strangers.

The directions: "The magic shop is a very special shop. You can get all kinds of things there for all kinds of prices. It has just one limitation: it only deals in human qualities. Oh, and one other one. Magic shopkeepers aren't interested in money. Not at all. They only barter. One human quality for another human quality. Are you beginning to understand? You can get whatever human quality appeals to you—anger, greed, kindness, humor, servility—if you're willing to pay the price. Before you begin, you need to know one more thing. The magic shop exists in someone's imagination. It needs a very specific location, the place you'd conjure up if you were to set up a store. We've had stores seven leagues under the sea run by an ancient sea serpent; a store set up in a clearing in the forest run by an age-old ageless shaman covered with leaves; stores in trees, on crags, in aeries. One shopkeeper was a spider who set up her shop in a corner of the cross of a medieval church in Cologne. If the shop has a clear location, it's easier for the clients to decide whether they want to shop there or not. And how to get there. The shaman in the forest had a hummingbird for a client, for example, who was bartering for relaxation. The spider was visited by a squirrel who couldn't be persuaded to give up any of his charm for the ability to express fury. Let's start by imagining where you'd set up your shop. Close your eyes if you want to. Get a very clear picture of the place. And of yourself in it. Where is your magic shop? What manner of shopkeeper are you?" I usually allow about three to five minutes. With these directions, everyone in the group has a participating experience in magic shop, and is thus far better equipped for further work than if he were to sit back and watch the performance of those few who are always ready to try something new. Here is an example of what may follow:

Leader: Who's got a shop all ready to go? Could you tell us about it?

John: The shop is in Muir Woods in an ancient redwood tree. Not in the tree but in the base, where a cave has been left by a fire near the roots.

Leader: Would you like to set it up?

John: O.K. (*The tree is fashioned from some chairs and pillows available in the room.*)

Leader: And who are you?

John: I'm a very cranky, irritable lizard. (*Group laughter. John is a very somber person and a staff member.*) But my shop is really full. I have everything everyone wants and a little more.

If the technique is used as a warm-up, the leader may want to stop at this point and ask others about their shops, each of which is, of course, a metaphor for the shopkeeper's existence. As a warm-up, the technique quickly provides a great deal of fellow feeling in a group willing and able to deal with the language of metaphor. If the leader wishes to set up a bargaining scene, he will continue:

Leader: How old a lizard are you?

John: Oh, I've been here since the fire, about 200 years ago, and I don't remember how old I was when I came.

Leader: O.K. You sound like a kind of scary storekeeper to me. But, there's probably someone here who wants to deal with you. People will go anywhere for a bargain. Who wants to go?

Mary: I do.

Leader: Who are you and how are you going to find John's tree in the forest?

Mary: Can I just be me?

Leader: It's better if you can use your imagination as well and find a shape and method of transportation that would fit the magic shop. Otherwise, how would you know about it?

Mary: Well, I go to this psychodrama group and. . . . O.K., O.K. Let's see . . . I'm a fawn. Just a little fawn traipsing through the forest. Everybody in the forest knows about the shop. So I'm just walking along.

Mary is a very pretty, fawnlike creature. The audience is delighted with her choice. The scene is now set up. From here on in, the leader's job is to see that active bargaining takes place. John is enjoying his role.

John: Good God! I hope I don't have any customers today! They're always messing things up. Urggg! (*Sticks his tongue out.*) I have a long sticky tongue. They'd better watch it. (*Disappears behind the pillows.*)

Mary (Having walked around the room a bit, she now pauses in front of the shop. Her voice is eager and friendly while the lizard remains terse and somewhat harsh except for momentary lapses): Knock, knock, anybody there?

John: I'm not going up there. This store isn't for children.

Mary: Knock, knock. Anybody there?

John (whispering and refusing to budge): No.

Mary: Hello there! I heard this is a magic shop. I want to trade with you.

John: Oh, alright then, have it your way (*appearing with his head out from under the chair*). What is it you want? Make it fast.

Mary: Well, I heard you bartered for human qualities here. Is that true?

John: Of course it's true.

Mary: I want some freedom. I want a whole lot of it. Do you have it here?

John: Of course I have it! But you'd better watch your tongue, I don't deal with doubters. What kind do you want?

Mary: I don't want to be so confined when I walk around the forest. I want to be free to go all over. I don't want to have to worry about the men with guns or the cars on the road. I want to be free.

John: What are you willing to give me in exchange? I have three fine cups of freedom, just the kind you want. What have you got?

Mary: I don't know . . . I'm just a young fawn. Do you know anything I have you want? What do you want? (*She is hesitant and somewhat embarrassed.*)

Like many magic shop customers, Mary has a great deal of difficulty answering the shopkeeper's question about her offer. Here the leader can provide some help:

Leader: Let's have some coaching from the audience, O.K.? Are there any other forest creatures here that want to kibbitz and make suggestions? (*Providing an example*) I'm a hawk and I say don't let that old lizard intimidate you, little fawn.

Group member: I'm another old lizard and I know we lizards need a lot of what you've got. Why don't you offer him some of your youth and beauty?

Mary: Oh no! I couldn't do that! That's me. I can't change who I am.

Group member: I'm a bird. Don't give him anything. You're fine the way you are.

Mary: Oh, he would just go away. (*Shopkeeper nods vigorously.*) And it really wouldn't be fair. . . . Let's see . . . Oh, I know! I'll give you some of my ability to jump over fences and bushes, my agility. But not all of it, I need some for myself. I'll give you one cup.

John: I'll take it. I'm agile enough, but I am getting older. What else have you got? Let's go. I'm tired of waiting.

Mary (suddenly lights up with a sense of real understanding): I know what I'll offer you. Something you really need. I'll offer you a cup of love. That's both loving and being loved. You *really* need that. Think how your life would change.

John (reacting with some surprise and smiles a rare smile): You got me . . . I really do need that. Few of my customers seem to have any to give. . . . A cup? . . . No, that's too little. I want all of it. Give me all of it and I'll give you all my freedom (*laughs*). I don't need any here in the tree, so I'm way ahead.

Mary: I can't do that. If I give you all my loving I'll just get old and crotchety like you. I don't want freedom that badly. What's the use of being free when you're all alone?

John (very cold): Let's cut the sermon. All or nothing.

Mary: Wouldn't you compromise?

John: No. All for all.

At this point, the leader may have to help the bargainers come to a conclusion. I usually find it helpful to continue to participate by role-playing an audience member:

Leader: We other forest animals demand that you bring this bargain to an end. This has gone far enough! (*Other group members join in readily, relieved they can express their impatience.*)

Group member: I'm a squirrel and I say, "Nuts to you." Go to another shop.

Group member: Yeah, this guy isn't going to give you any bargain. Leave.

Mary: Well, it doesn't look like I'll get what I want. . . . I'll have to go. . . . But I'm really sad. . . . Are you sure?

John: Of course I am.

Mary: I don't like it. I'll have to keep my guard up. Be careful. Watch that I don't get hurt. But at least I'll get some loving.(*Leaves slowly.*)

Like many of life's choices, many magic shop encounters luckily remain unresolved. For our purposes, resolution is of little importance. The metaphoric content and the process of bargaining provide a rich soil for exploration of the self. The group's response to the metaphor is usually automatic, needing little framing or encouraging from the leader. John's gruffness was easily recognized by others as the quality that made it difficult for other staff members and patients alike to get a word with him in his office. His apparent recognition of his lack of warmth was enthusiastically received by the group—if he could admit it, maybe he wasn't quite so bad. Mary's characterization of herself as a pretty, vulnerable, naive creature of the forest seemed completely congruent to those of us who knew her.

After a magic shop scene is concluded, I usually try to focus on the bargaining process by asking, "How did you feel the bargaining went? What kind of bargainers did you see?"

In our scene, John responded immediately. Looking around at the downcast and exasperated expressions of the faces of several group members, he said, somewhat sadly, "Well, that's what my wife says about me, too. All or nothing. I just can't compromise. She could sure see me as a cranky old lizard who lives all by himself."

Most of the group members had sided with Mary and were a little surprised when she also expressed some sadness about her way of bargaining. "This is the way it always happens. I talk and talk and then nothing changes. I don't know why I always seem to choose guys like that old lizard to bargain with."

The next stage of the psychodrama involves planning further work. I may ask the bargainers, "Now what do you want to do? Mary, do you want to explore another way of bargaining with a double?" Or we may want to work with John. "John, how about choosing someone to play the role of your wife and going home to tell her about today's magic shop?"

John was eager to work. Mary was not. The rest of the work with John was a scene with his wife where he and his double explored ways of escaping the "all-or-nothing" bind. John's stubbornness, together with his realization of the loneliness which ensued, provided a poignant experience and touched off several other magic shops in which the barter centered on love. If the magic shop develops into a successful bargain—a mouse, for example, is able to trade some of her ability to look helpless for an ounce of social poise—I may want to continue by asking, "What are you going to do differently now? Now that you have that ounce of poise, whom do you want to encounter?" Again, the answers will provide guidelines for further scenes.

The role of the shopkeeper can be played with two quite different strategies. The first strategy is the one naturally picked by two inexperienced players, and demonstrated by our cranky lizard. In it, the shopkeeper, like the shopper, bargains for what he himself wants and needs. Both shopkeeper and shopper learn something about the ways in which each wants to change and what the costs of such change might be. In the second strategy, the shopkeeper uses his position to show the shopper something new and surprising about the bargain he wants to drive:

He: I'm a beautiful golden statue of the Buddha.

She: I know, and I'm a butterfly. I'm just as beautiful as you are and I want strength.

He: What kind of strength?

She: Strength to oppose the wind and to wrench open the mouths of chameleons that want to eat me.

He: I'll give you some strength but you won't always know when it comes.

She: What do you mean?

He: Sometimes you'll be able to oppose the wind alright, but sometimes you'll just want to brush someone with your lovely wings and it will hurt them.

Our butterfly now has to consider giving up the knowledge of her own harmlessness. The clever shopkeeper has provided her with a real-life risk. A snail who wants to be explosive must realize that he risks exploding his own shell. A hummingbird who desires peacefulness may need to know that he will have to give up some of his ability to move at an instant's notice. The mole who wants to bargain for sociability and friendship may have to give up some of his ability to dig himself into a deep private hole.

The essence of this type of magic shop is the setting up of a bargain during which it becomes irrevocably clear that the shopper *does not want to* (in contrast to: isn't able to, cannot, doesn't have a chance to) obtain the quality he seeks because it means giving up something crucial in return. It is often helpful if the shopkeeper is a therapist, someone in a position to know what the shopper might have to give up in order to gain what he wants.

One of my favorite fairy tales in early childhood was the tale of the princess who couldn't stop crying. With the help of a witch who lived at the end of an arduous trail in one of the princess's forests, she traded her tears in for laughter and a necklace. The bargain was a poor one—our princess had wanted to laugh instead of cry. Now, everytime she found herself in a situation which would formerly have moved her to tears, she laughed, laughed as uncontrollably as she had cried before, and the necklace of beads seemed to dance and jingle along. Needless to say, she spent another goodly portion of her life on that same arduous trail through the forest until she found the witch and returned the fatal necklace. Our magic shopkeepers often encounter princesses with equally foolish wishes. We hope, through the bargaining, to increase their wisdom by a degree. Some examples of the technique follow.

Burt is a longstanding member of one of our couples' groups. He is a mild-mannered, gentle, youngish man who speaks in a soft, appealing voice. The group has long seen the underside of his smooth exterior. Burt is our champion procrastinator. He is as stubborn as a mule. He asks for help with the most charming of appeals. But he will not move. Any suggestion is seen as a demand. He won't respond to demands. And he doesn't know what he could do on his own. So he doesn't move. He has come to my magic shop asking to buy the ability to work. He has no job. His wife is tired of supporting the family and he feels she has a point. But he can't get himself to do anything. He can't do the little jobs that need doing around the house; he can't seem to work on his art projects; he can't think what job he might seek. He sighs. I ask him what he's offering in exchange for the quality he wants. I know already what I want and I'm waiting for the right moment to pounce.

He offers me some pride. I take some, saying he'll need some for later and I add wryly that I'm not too interested in pride, especially in the absence of real achievements. Burt and I know each other well enough to allow some bantering. He offers me a little of his creativity. The other group members counsel him against giving me any of it. I say I don't have that much demand for creativity without joy, anyway. I take a pound, again without much enthusiasm. I'm a very snooty shopkeeper. He offers me some enthusiastic self-confidence, the feeling, when he starts, that whatever he's doing is going to be terrific, the best of its kind. I accept. He still hasn't come up with what I want. I take two cups of confidence. He can't think what I want. He doesn't have anything else to offer. He looks wan. Full of self-pity. Status quo.

I begin my pounce. "How about your freedom of choice? Your freedom to do whatever you want all day long?"

He reacts very quickly, with a mixture of surprise and anger. Then he smiles, "Wow, my first reaction was you can't have *any* of that!"

I pounce. "I want all of it. Well, almost all—99% of what you have." The bargain is on. He can't understand that any human being should be asked to give up freedom of any kind. I let him know that I need a lot of it since a lot of people have given up so much of it that they'll barter some of their most valuable properties for very small amounts. I also let him know that I think he will still be well-endowed with freedom of choice about his daily schedule even if he gives me 99% of what he has. He will still have more than most people he knows.

He asks a lot of questions. He offers nothing. There is no bargain.

After a week has passed, at the next group meeting, Burt comes back to my magic shop. He has changed his mind. His freedom isn't doing him all that much good anyway. He just broods and aches with it. He'll take the bargain. The group members are enthused. They take advantage of the chance to talk to Burt about his activities; for once, he doesn't seem put off by them. My co-therapist suggests testing Burt's resolution by actually letting some of the group members check on his activities. Burt likes the idea. He is to receive a phone call at the end of each day for the next week, during which he is to account for his day's work. The following week, Burt appears more energized and reports a great improvement in his productivity. For the time being, he has worked himself out of his impasse.

Barbara, a young woman in her early twenties who is a member of an individuals' group at our center, came to my shop wanting the ability to handle her class of 5th graders more successfully. We had already spent some time role-playing her class, and, as 5th graders, immediately found our teacher's weak spot. She took everything personally. We were just kids doing whatever we could to amuse ourselves in a boring situation. And it was easy to amuse ourselves with our teacher because she got uptight at the slightest provocation. Her face got all tense. She threatened punishments she didn't carry through. Mostly, it was her voice, though. She whined as though she was appealing to us in some weird way. What a drag.

In my magic shop, Barbara offered her intelligence, her discipline, her depression, her creativity, as I bided my time for the pounce. This time it was: "Will you give up the hope that the kids in your class are going to make you feel like a good person?"

Again, the instantaneous reaction. Barbara clutched her stomach and said, "My first thought is, no, you just can't take *that* away from me." We bargained awhile. I let her know— zen-master fashion—that only in giving it up might she gain what she wanted; that being a good person might be the subject for another magic shop.

Barbara did not make a bargain. She is still thinking about it.

A magic shop bargain can be amazingly effective. In one instance, a young man who had been subsisting on welfare payments because of his inability to find work chose to go to a magic shop run by an ancient Tibetan Lama who lived high up in the mountains in a city carved out of rock by his loyal followers. In order to get there, he disguised himself as a mountain goat—skittish, lacking in patience, but strong and lithe enough to scale the most difficult of mountain terrains.

Lama: What do you want?

Goat: I want to be able to hold a job. I want some confidence and some patience so I can stay put instead of jumping and bolting at the slightest perturbance.

Lama: What do you offer me in return?

Goat: I don't have much. I could offer you some skittishness. Somebody who had trouble smelling danger could use it, maybe. I have no trouble with that at all.

Lama: Sadly enough, I have a lot of that quality already. Many of my customers lately seem to have an oversupply. But

I could use a cupful. It would hardly make a dent in your stock, I'm afraid.

Goat: Then I'd need a really large supply of confidence to last out all those situations where I get scared. I need an ocean of confidence and all I've offered you is a cupful of skittishness. Could you use my ability to survive on very little? I've been living on welfare for more than a year now.

Lama: I could use that. In this materialistic age, it's a sought-after quality. Will you give me all of yours?

Goat: No, I still might need it sometime. I'll give you 75%, how's that?

Lama: I'll take it.

Goat: Is it enough?

Lama: No.

Goat: Do you see anything else you want?

Lama: I want your helplessness. It's a very effective variety. You've been able to get others to give you food, money, therapy. A lot of my customers need that variety of helplessness. And you won't need it anymore if you have confidence and patience, so give me all of it.

Goat: All of it? Then I'll never be able to get any help if I need it. No. I'll give you 75% again, is that enough?

Lama: It's a bargain, if you want it. An ocean of confidence and patience for a cupful of skittishness and 75% of both your ability to survive on very little and your ability to be effectively helpless.

Goat: I'm afraid it'll be pretty scary sometimes, but I accept.

The bargain had the best of consequences. The young man took his confidence job-hunting with him, landed a job, and kept it for the entire following year. In fact, he may still have it, as the writer has heard nothing to the contrary.

Some of the best magic shop bargains end without resolution. In that case, the magic shop often serves to clarify an impasse in a dramatic, experiential way. The shopper may need to return to his impasse again and again before he can see his way clear to resolving it. Meanwhile, the bargaining continues, in one way or another.

The magic shop is a special technique: it is playful, sensitive, poetic. And it has all the disadvantages of other such animals. Mood and atmosphere have to be right. The group has to be verbal and willing to play. The more imaginative the group—college kids, teachers, therapists, artists, children— the more likely the success. When the group aura is one of "sound scientific reasoning," "onions and potatoes," "no nonsense," or other exclusively hard-nosed approaches to psychotherapy, it will be more difficult to run a magic shop. Group members may have to get over a feeling of being condescended to or infantilized by the leader; others may become bored with the somewhat abstract nature of the bargaining. The magic shop is a powerful technique, but limited. The time must be right. It can't be repeated very often.

Chapter 11

Masks

I first encountered the use of masks through Bari Rolfe, a modern dancer who had developed the art of mime as a tool for drama students. The mime's primary organ of emotional expression is his body. Often, he makes sure that it is his body that "speaks" by painting his face a stark white and wearing a very understated costume. He keeps his face very still. Bari uses another method to eliminate the language of the face and enhance the expression of the body. The face is covered by one unvarying expression: the expression of the mask.

Masks can represent any of the basic polarities of human expression: youth–age; seriousness–foolishness; beauty–ugliness; meanness–kindness; coldness–warmth. Bari works with one additional mask: the universal mask, a mask designed to suggest only common humanity. The universal mask is neutral in

117

skin tone; the features are classical and somewhat bland. Its nearest relative is the face of an unmade-up storeroom dummy; it suggests neither comedy nor tragedy. Even more than the expressionless face of the mime, this mask gains meaning only through the movement of the wearer.

When Bari began a series of classes for a group of therapists interested in developing the mask as an experiential tool, I joined. I found that she worked very much in the way I had in my first psychodrama group. She gave us the same exercises which she used with her actors and dancers, in the hope that we would find our own application. All of these exercises can easily be used as a warm-up and then developed for a psychodrama.

We began very simply. A trunk full of fifteen or twenty masks* was brought to our group room, from which all the furniture had been removed. Instead of the usual assortment of pillows and lamps, the room was bare save for a full-length mirror brought in especially for the exercises. Bari suggested that we examine the masks and choose one that appealed to us, any mask that struck an emotional chord. We were then encouraged to try on the mask, to work with it in front of the mirror, to move our heads and upper bodies in ways that seemed to suit the mask, and, finally, to find the mask's walk.

The masks looked rather small and unassuming at first sight. They were a grayish white or skin color. Their expressions were extreme and often grotesque. I thought, as I put mine on, that it would never fit my face; it seemed out of proportion, the wrong color—in short, incongruous. As I moved it around, adjusting it to my face and hair, I soon changed my mind. It became a part of me quite easily. And, as I looked at the others in the room, half-expecting an embarrassing version of Halloween, I saw that they were fitting into their masks as well.

---

*Masks are easily made. The simplest instructions can be found in any book on the use of papier-mâché. Halloween masks, pie tins, and those fiberglass forms found in equipment packages serve easily as molds. Books on theater arts give further instructions in the use of lighter, plastic materials for making masks by taking impressions of actual faces, storeroom dummy faces, or other masks. In our own group, we spent two delightful Saturday afternoons making masks—an activity which in itself spurs the imagination and helps build group solidarity.

All of the therapists in the room knew each other well. We began to experiment with new body positions and movements to fit our masks. I was startled that the others around me seemed to have become strangers. When I looked in the mirror, I found myself quite unrecognizable as well.

I had chosen the mask of an old, wrinkled person with an expression that seemed to me to be discouraged and at the same time forbearing. The mask was considerably larger than my own face. As I began to arrange my hair around it in an effort to make it look more natural, I found myself feeling heavier and sadder. My head drooped further forward. My back rounded. My elbows locked at my sides, leaving only my forearms and hands to make some rather futile, small gestures. I walked slowly. When I encountered other maskers I felt like the eternal mother: touching people lightly, making some clucking noises that seemed both old and very young, shaking my head in what seemed both an affirmation of the other person and a resignation to my own burdensome existence. The mood is not a familiar one to me. I am a person who normally moves quickly, moves past people, stopping only if I have a reason. Mine is an aggressive, rather than a resigned stance, yet putting on the mask had created this mood perfectly. I had become a composite of many of the old women I had known.

All of us had the experience of not quite recognizing the others. The mask simplified our perception of the others much as does a videotape with the sound turned off. Only in this case we are not only deprived of the voice of the familiar person, but also of another basis for recognizing the other's mood: changes of facial expression. Just as many of us find out over and over again that we rely on words and thoughts to give us information about the world and therefore fail to comprehend much of the emotional output which is coming our way, so many of us during this exercise became aware of being face-watchers. What a shock to be confronted with an unmoving face! Some of us missed the subtlety of the others' expressions so much that we began to swear that the masks *were* changing—raising an eyebrow, pulling down a corner of the mouth, etc.! We became so hungry for a facial expression that we were reading into the mask what we saw in the expression of the body.

The uses of this very simple exercise seem to me to be at least three. First, the mask, like the magic shop, gives permission to the wearer to experiment with a fantasy. This may be the most important function of many of the psychodrama techniques and it will be discussed more fully later. Second, the wearer finds himself disguised in a way that affords him new insight into the way his body moves. His body, displayed against the unfamiliarity of the mask, becomes newly visible. Third, the wearer of the mask experiences a marked change in the reactions of others to him. We often forget that we are as accustomed to the responses we elicit as to those we give. We're not only accustomed to acting a certain way, but we rely on others to react to us in a certain way as well. The mask enables the wearer to experience himself in a new context.

Throughout Europe, where I grew up, there are traditional celebrations where masks are worn. The Bavarian *Fashing* lasts for several days; the masked ball only an evening; the Tyrolean peasants' *Walpurgisnacht*, one whole night. The folklore of many European localities which enjoy such celebrations contains volumes of tales of the adventure, trickery, and supernatural revelations occurring to the maskers. I had often pondered the functions and delights of these emotionally charged events, which have an obvious appeal to the psychodramatist. Clearly, they provide a chance for revelry and new flirtation. They provide an opportunity for the expression of fantasy. Many a child (and many an adult) has seen a part of a familiar tale come true on these nights.

It was through our work with masks, however, that I learned a new and very important lesson about the experience of the masquerader: he has the opportunity of stepping into another life. He can move, sense, and see differently. He can experiment with being another person as far removed from his everyday self as he chooses. And, perhaps most important, others will respond to him quite differently. No other form of self-disguise is so successful. Masked, he will experience not being recognized by those who know him. He will experience others reacting to a different person inside his own skin.

In our next exercise, we used the universal mask. Our object was to make our movements congruent with its universality; in short, to portray Everyman.

Exercise for Use of Universal Mask

Directions: "I want you to be a human being who existed much earlier in time, in much more primitive conditions. You will be alone. You have spent a night sleeping in the forest. This is the time when you awaken. Remember that what we want to see is what might be the most basic characteristic of any human being in this situation. We're not interested in particularities such as whether the person is happy or unhappy, how old he is, whether he has a headache. Just give us the basics. What does he experience, see, touch? How does he move? It will help you if you concentrate on your surroundings and react to them in the most simple, economical way you can."

Again, I will relate my own experience in using this mask. Its immediate effect is to blank out the face and enhance the body. As I looked at myself wearing the regular-featured, classically neutral mask, I found myself immediately much more aware of my body movement. Because the face told me nothing in particular, I was able to look at the way I moved with the kind of objectivity I usually reserve for viewing others. As I looked in the mirror, I thought: *My shoulders tend to draw up. I think I'll let them down. What an erect position! Isn't that a little stiff? Try to relax some, generally, Eva. Why carry one hand in front of your body as though you're carrying a purse? There is no reason why you can't just let your arms drop to your sides. . . . There is no reason to walk so hesitantly. Just walk.* Gradually, I eliminated some of the peculiarities of my own ways of moving.

As the exercise continued and I had some measure of success, there was a great sense of achievement and pleasure. Partly, this was a function of the type of movement I chose to fit the mask and the exercise. I had relaxed. There was a freshness and sensual pleasure in performing the exercise of awakening in the forest on a warm summer day. And there was one further quality which delighted me and which, I have since found, delights many patients. It was the experience of projecting something basically human, an experience akin to "belonging," the reverse of the alienation and differentness I had carried with me so much of my life.

As we continued to work with the masks, the exercises became more and more complex. We each explored the use of different masks—different selves—working out short improvisations suggested by the masks individually, with one or two partners, or as a group. The usual acting exercises employed in group improvisations work equally well with masks. After everyone in the group has selected a mask, the group is told that, for example, they will spend the next twenty minutes portraying people caught in an air-raid shelter during World War II, or in the waiting room of a doctor's office, or at a once-a-year bargain-basement sale in a large city. There is, of course, one very important difference between the masked improvisations and other acting exercises: the mask demands silence. All communication has to be mimed.

I would not use the masks with a group composed of individuals of low ego-strength or individuals who, for some other reason, have little tolerance for the use and expression of their imagination. For such people, the mask is threatening. The visual effect alone can be bewildering. Masks can increase resistances by increasing the fear of ridicule, embarrassment, and humiliation.

Mask Exercise in Couples' Group

Another of the exercises with masks may be used with married couples. The couple is instructed to find character masks which illustrate some aspect of each partner's experience in the relationship. I recall vividly my own experience in doing this exercise with my husband.

As we went up to the trunkful of masks, I already knew which mask I'd choose. It was a mask I'd worn for years as a teenager and young woman, a mask that had taken a great deal of hard work to shake off, one that still returned in times of stress. The mask seemed little. Its most prominent feature was a grin. A very large grin. Every other feature of the face was tyrannized by that grin, which seemed to spread from ear to ear. The forehead was wrinkled, there were deep furrows at the sides of the mouth, and the small round eyes were barely visible beneath the folds of the all-encompassing smile.

Alan, meanwhile, had chosen a mask as well. In some ways, it was the opposite of mine. Where mine showed a small face, his was large; mine was wrinkled, his quite smooth. While mine could have been either a woman's or a man's face, his was decidedly masculine. When I first looked at him with the mask on, he appeared to me to be the classic villain. The mask's smooth, large face was highlighted by prominent cheekbones and rather small, slitty eyes. The mouth was thin and, to my view, menacing. The most striking aspect of the mask was its blankness—it was smooth, cold, and lacking in any kind of emotional responsiveness.

Our task was to relate to each other for a few minutes wearing these masks and to use them to bring out the part of ourselves which they represented to us. We began the exercise. I, of course, slid very easily into my familiar part. I began to "make nice." My object was to be cheerful, to help out, to put a good face on things (a fitting metaphor indeed), to help Alan and myself stay in a sort of pleasant limbo which would keep any strong emotion from being felt.

As I flitted about, touching Alan here and there, bringing him some food, chucking him under the chin, miming my little cheerfulness, I found to my surprise that he was portraying a character who was not in the least menacing. In fact, as he continued, I realized that a menace would have been a relief in comparison to the character he was playing. He was playing a passive, docile, and helpless person. The more I flitted, the more he sagged. He seemed not to know what to do about anything. He required help and explanation in order to eat, to plan the next activity, and then, when we were doing that activity, to execute it. After our snack, I showed my help-less friend that I wanted him to help me with the dishes. Slow-ly, he got the idea. Then he started dropping dishes. He didn't know where to put them when he had dried them. And he looked more and more sad and helpless. He never laughed at my jokes.

Little did I know at the outset of our improvisation with what vehemence I would be thrust back into my old "cheery rescuer" self. I very quickly ceased playing a role. The more helpless Alan looked, the more frantic I felt inside. I *had* to cheer him up. I couldn't leave him to his own devices. I couldn't for a moment let either of us see who he was without help or who I was without helping. I rushed about, compul-sively taking charge of both our actions and glossing over his failures when they occurred.

The members of our group (all of whom knew each other and the two of us quite well) responded to our scene with a good deal of laughter. The extremes of our positions had been true for us in some of the other ways that they'd known us. The miming presented them in a comic form. For Alan and me, the exercise still serves as a reminder of one of the ways we get into trouble under stress.

The directions I use for the couples' exercise with masks are as follows:

Directions: "I would like each of you to select a mask which has some meaning to you in terms of your relationship to your husband or wife. Needless to say, this is a nonverbal ex-ercise and the mask selection is to be done without talking. When each of you has put on your mask, I want you to mime some regular household activity together. It doesn't matter who starts; the other will get the idea of what you're doing and will join you. Remember the mask you are wear-ing and behave in the way the mask directs you to behave. We will take four or five minutes for this exercise."

The couples' exercise can be used both in a group and during a regular clinical hour. One can elaborate the exercise in sev-eral ways, always using both mirror and video-feedback to help people see themselves. (1) We ask members of each couple to select masks for each other, and then perform the same exercise. (2) Each couple is asked to select masks representing different aspects of their relationship: harmony, disharmony, the relationship at an earlier time, in the future, if worst comes to worst, etc.

In our couples' group, we found the two elaborations of the technique to be particularly fruitful in testing projections. The husband who put a particularly bitter mask on his wife, for example, found, as she began to play her scene with him, that he no longer experienced her in this way, that the bitterness of her mask was familiar, but as a memory of the past. The mask no longer fit her. Another couple surprised many in the group when the wife selected a strong, rather athletic-looking mask—a mask that would have been perfect for a football player—as the mask she would like to see her husband wear. She had spent much of the group's time complaining about his lack of emotionality. Now she seemed to be making a statement that it was she who preferred the strong, silent type.

Each exercise can be developed further. For example, when there is a large response to a particular scene in the couples' group, we often ask other couples to do exercises using the same masks. In that way we can look at some of the ingredients of many of the archetypal marital conflicts: introvert–extrovert, witch–victim, villain–victim, victim–rescuer, stoneface–hysteric, etc. An exercise can be made more intense by asking the players to redo a scene, pushing it to its logical extreme: "If this mask represented your life for the next ten years, how do you two think you'd be relating to each other then? Let's see you ten years later." When using these instructions to intensify a particular experience, it is important to allow the individuals involved time in which they can concentrate on what has already happened, so that they will know what feelings and sensations to exaggerate.

Directions: "Before you start, give yourself a few minutes to take stock of your present state of mind. How do you feel now, at the end of this scene? What feels familiar? What

feels strange? What is your mood like? What do you feel toward your partner? What is your body telling you? Are you
feeling tense or relaxed? If you are tense, where is the tension located? If you exaggerated that tension more and
more, what would happen to your body? Close your eyes, if
you wish, and let yourself answer these questions. Think
and feel what might happen to you after ten more years of
this kind of existence. In a few minutes, we'll take a look at
you two as you would be ten years later."

This method of intensification is applicable to many of the
techniques described in this book. An individual who has arranged a sociogram can be asked to relate to those same individuals after ten years of similar interactions with them, for
example. A group doing a drawing together for a warm-up exercise can be asked to take stock of themselves and fantasize
where ten years of similar interrelationships would lead them.
In fact, any scene representing an important relationship can
be explored further with this type of dramatic intensification.

In using these exercises with various groups of patients, I
have come to think that they are of particular value to groups
composed of individuals with a high degree of verbal skills.
They have all the advantages of other nonverbal exercises in
breaking through the verbal, intellectualizing defenses and, in
addition, they appear to provide an unusually potent catalyst
for the use of the imagination. For individuals who are flexible
and confident enough not to be threatened by the sheer outra-
geousness of a room full of people disguised by grotesque
masks, these group exercises are energizing. Frequently, they
even lead to that process so little known in the hallowed halls
of group therapy: having fun.

Chapter 12

Permission
for Spontaneity

We clinicians are inundated with bad news. Our patients come to us with tales of woe about the past and tales of sorrow about the present. So often we are called upon to listen, to help our patients make sense of what is happening to them, to support them, that sometimes we forget that we have another role altogether, a role which is equally health-giving and not nearly so depressing. We can provide a new context for our patients, a context where both patient and therapist can experiment with different roles, however much their initial timidity may enjoin them against it.

If we let our office walls be party only to the sadness of the past and the hopelessness of the present, we ourselves will soon become depleted of whatever small amount of healing power has been given us. If, on the other hand, four office walls can be changed at will to a carnival, to another planet, to a submarine, then there's some hope that something different can occur both for ourselves and for our patients, something nurturing supplied through energy which is released when the imagination is put to use and fantasies are acted out.

Both clinician and patient live in a world where a sort of dreary sense of responsibility is paraded constantly and spontaneity is feared and suppressed. At worst, the clinician often finds himself rigidly bound by a picture of A Therapist: a quietly dressed, soft-spoken, kindly but slightly impersonal individual who is careful to use no language of any color and who is limited to either short questions or short answers when talking to his patient. All too frequently, his Patient is equally bound. He knows that he is to come in and talk about problems. He cultivates a downcast expression, a thoughtful brow, often speaks even more softly than his therapist (the therapist seems to be giving the message that talking up is wrong somehow), and cannot imagine saying that anything good is happening in his life or engaging the therapist by telling a joke, for example. (Well, perhaps he can imagine it, but he knows better than to try it.) Both therapist and patient have many, many fantasies, intuitions, and associations during the hour which are well within their awareness but which they know to be inappropriate to the context of the lofty work in which they are engaged. Needless to say, these are stereotypes, and they do not exist only in individual therapy; they exist in groups, in families, in all aspects of our lives.

The user of psychodrama is the enemy of the constricting stereotype. He's an iconoclast. He frequently does the unexpected and asks his patients to do the same. He gives permission to be spontaneous, to experiment, to try out something ludicrous, something potentially embarrassing, something new. We have talked about the kind of information derived from the clinical use made of such techniques as doubling, role reversal, the magic shop, and the use of masks, but we have not talked enough about the powerful message given by the purveyor of these techniques. (Of course not; if we were going to intrigue any timid clinicians, we didn't want to frighten them away in the beginning.)

A therapist who starts talking about a shop that deals in human qualities, who owns a trunkful of strange masks, who suddenly gets up and talks for another person as though he were part of him, is modeling a spontaneity which will be one of the most valuable assets his patient could gain in the process of working with him. He is giving permission to play. He is giving permission to talk and listen at several levels: the level of content and information, the level of drama, the level of fantasy, and the level of play. By participating in some of the scenes he sets up, he is modeling a way out of the tales of woe, a way to take an active part, a way that may prove to be enjoyable, exciting, even fear-provoking. He is giving permission to experiment, to play, and to change.

We often think of all forms of therapy as forms of re-parenting. The therapist who can play is clearly one of the most enjoyable substitute parents an individual could want. He will encourage his child to grow, to be different, and he will be able to model both the excitement of play and of serious intensity in his therapeutic relationship.

Chapter 13

Resistances and Some Ways of Dealing with Them

The basic resistance is always the same: the fear of change. We want to become different but we dread it. Whether we are confronting helpful friends or relatives, a priest, a therapist, or a group, there's always a part of each of us that wants to experiment, to risk, to venture forth into the unknown, and part that holds back—conservative, frightened, paranoid—quick to judge the risk foolish, ridiculous, contemptible.

Role-playing presents a special kind of risk. It entails taking a chance on "being" someone else and it entails performing this process in front of others. The basic resistances specific to the process of psychodrama involve fears relating to the actual playing of a role, i.e., fears of losing the familiar sense of self.

131

Idiosyncrasies such as tone of voice, quality of language, gestures, and rhythm of movement help each of us identify ourselves. At times of stress we cling with desperation to our identifying characteristics. It is hard to risk trying to act differently. The thought of acting the role of another person may have great appeal—it offers a rich soil for trying out aspects of ourselves we've neglected—yet we resist, afraid that somehow the old self won't be the same thereafter, afraid of the unknown self which may emerge.

The question "Who am I" looms large on our alienated horizon; role-playing often appears as a threat. *Does playing a role well mean that the real self is finally emerging? What if I like myself better the way I usually am? One way to handle it is just to play nice people. That way I won't take a chance. Another way is not to take part at all—"I'm just watching."*

When in doubt, say, "I can't." It's a nice way of saying "I won't"; it lets both of us off the hook. If I can't do it—well, that means I would if I could. And you obviously can't ask me to do something I'm unable to do.

The "I can't" is a familiar maneuver in any resistance game. In psychodrama, the "I can't" usually refers to the technique of role-playing. The individual knows that "he can't do it." He is not skilled enough, not smart enough, not brazen enough. He is embarrassed. He appears to have stage fright. *I can't act; I can only be myself. . . . I couldn't do that in front of all these people. . . . I don't know how she's feeling, how could I act like her? . . . I never even met his mother, I can't be her. . . . I'm too embarrassed to try.*

A person who feels very threatened by the thought of role-playing may resist in another way, by questioning its basis or attacking it as a harmful activity. *Role-playing is a game which will only teach me to play more artificial games. Role-playing is dangerous because it will distort my view of reality and drive me crazy.*

Both types of resistance present serious problems to the psychodrama leader because, as all of us who have led other types of groups well know, resistance is highly infectious. *If he can't do it; I can't do it. If he says it's bad for us, maybe it is bad for us*. It is important, thus, to consider these questions and arrive at some ways of handling them.

The warm-up is the most valuable antidote to resistance. No amount of explanation can supplant the simple messages given by a successful warm-up: this is a group where everyone can participate; participation is easy and fun; any contribution is rewarded. In structuring the warm-up, the leader gives the message that he is prepared to take a lot of responsibility for the functioning of the group. A group member is not left to his own devices, struggling with his own fears. The warm-up sets up an atmosphere of spontaneity which runs counter to the resistive trends in the group and does much to neutralize them. At the end of the warm-up, most of the group members will have participated to some degree or "broken the ice," while the remainder have learned that they will not be punished for resisting, but rather encouraged to participate until they are ready to do so.

In struggling with my own inner resistances—my timidity, if you will—and those of group members, especially those groups of people which I see in acute states of crisis on hospital wards or in day centers, I have developed a style which is at some variance with "classical" or Moreno-style psychodrama. It consists largely of techniques which de-emphasize the aspect of "theater" or "staginess" in psychodrama and attempt to replace these with a concept of psychotherapeutic work more akin to the atmosphere of other therapy groups. The stage area can be anywhere in the room; it is usually either in the center of the circle around which we sit, or is even part of it. There is no "stage." If a person doesn't want to work in the middle of the room, I usually move the stage area to wherever he happens to be sitting and work from there. I may direct sitting next to him, to give him extra support. Neither is a "performance" required. If others can't hear the protagonists, I usually ask them to move nearer the area where he is working rather than asking him to speak louder. I don't want to ask the protagonist to "technically" produce his feelings in a louder voice than is comfortable for him, and I have no objection to others sitting near him, on the floor, even if it doesn't quite fit the scene. I discourage applause because I don't want to give group members the message that they have to be entertaining or entertained by what's going on. An empathic comment or a hug is a far more personal and supportive communication than the clapping of hands. Following a scene in a small group, it is often possible to ask each member what touched him about the drama he just saw. This technique provides both an emotional outlet for the observers and an opportunity for the protagonists to hear strongly felt commentary.

These techniques do much to counter the "I can't" resistance. All of them continue the message of the warm-up that anyone can participate, that there will be support from the leader, and that no specialized skills are required. The leader's own attitude to the "I can't" resistance is very important. If he hears it as a statement of fact or a final evaluation of the person's abilities, he's obviously lost. If he can hear it as information about the person's present state of mind in relation to trying a new and threatening activity, he can begin to work. I usually assume that the person "can" and doesn't know it. If a group member responds to a request to play a role by saying something like, "Oh, no! I couldn't do that. Pick somebody else," I usually respond in a very low-keyed manner intended to convey that I do not want to do battle about whether she is to participate, but rather that I want to help her to give herself a chance to try. I may use any number of the following phrases: "Well, let's see, maybe you could give it a try, knowing that it's hard to start. You don't know yet whether or not you can do it . . . it just feels like it might be hard." I may then also make some suggestions which will help give the individual more control over her choice and counteract her feeling that she is making a fool of herself, as in the following, where Joan is reluctant to participate:

Leader: "Could you try it if John showed you what his wife was like by playing the role himself first?"

Leader (to John): "John, you're Mary. How old a woman are you? Have you been married to John for a long time? What's it like to be married to John?"

Leader (to Joan): "How about trying it and letting John decide how you're doing?"

Leader (to John): "John, if the way Joan plays your wife doesn't fit, will you stop the scene and let her know?"

Leader (to Joan): "Could you try it for a little while and then stop to consider whether you want to continue or get a replacement from the group?"

Leader (to Joan): "Are you saying 'I can't' or 'I won't'? If you really mean 'I won't,' then there's nothing more I want to say to you right now; you'll just experience it as pressure. Try saying it to me."

Joan: "What do you mean?"

Leader: "Say, 'I won't' to me, to see if it fits for you."

Joan: "O.K. Yeah, that's right. I won't do it. I don't want to do what you asked. I won't."

Leader: "O.K. You won't."

The individual may then be able to say more about not wanting to participate. I will usually come back to her later to keep checking to see if other circumstances increase her desire to participate. In the event that the individual sticks to her original "I can't," I assume that she is telling me that she wants to try, and any of the above techniques becomes applicable. During this discussion I watch closely for any signs that indicate that Joan may be willing to change her mind. If I see her nodding her head, smiling, or making a move into the scene with John, I usually encourage her by remaining near her physically until she feels more comfortable. It very seldom happens that the individual uses the controls offered to her— to stop and ask for help, or stop and get a replacement. However, if she does, I make very sure that we follow through on our contract. In general, I assume that group members attend because they want to try and because they want to participate. If the assumption proves false with a particular individual, I try to communicate two messages: that it's O.K. not to want to participate and that there'll be further opportunity to try in case he changes his mind. For example:

John: I think this is ridiculous (*sounding very belligerent*). The other therapists here are trying to teach us to be more realistic and this is phony. It's artificial.

Eva: That's true, it's artificial. It's a way of exploring by doing something artificial.

John: Well, *I'm* not going to do it. It isn't going to help me, I don't think.

Eva: That's O.K. I'll probably come back to you every once in a while though, to see if you want to participate. Is that O.K. with you?

John: (*nods head* 'yes' *reluctantly*).

If John had not given his reluctant assent in the end, I would have accepted that response as well, asking him to stay around to see how the rest of it went. This strategy allows John to take a negative position without being punished for it, and saves the leader from getting into a struggle with John which would infect the rest of the group members.

When, like John, the resisting individual questions role-playing itself, some discussion may be in order. He may feel it's all phony or artificial or he may make a learned disputation on the impossibility of ever stepping into anyone else's shoes. His quarrel is not with his lack of ability to perform the task; he is stating his opposition to the very concept of psychodrama as a healing art. I have formulated my thoughts on these issues in the following monologue, which forms my own personal basis for the points I want to make in a discussion of these issues:

"I am who I am. Psychodrama can't suddenly change that. I can't become someone else. I am who I am. I can, however, use various parts of myself to play different roles. Some of those parts may be close to what you already know of me. If I play Jane's girl friend, talking to her about why I think nobody else in the dormitory likes us, you may see very little difference from the Eva that leads psychodrama. A little softer maybe, a little more circumstantial and chatty in her conversation. But pretty much the same Eva. If I play John's wife, accusing him of hurting my feelings, you will see an Eva that seldom appears in Eva, the psychodrama leader, but you won't be terribly surprised. 'That's just the way she acts at home. She doesn't get that upset with us. Because we don't have that kind of power in her life,' you might think. You're right. I know the Eva I bring out when I play John's wife very well. My high-pitched, somewhat whiny voice. My tendency to say the same thing over and over. My injured air. But I don't usually trot this part of myself out in public.

"Neither Jane's girl friend nor John's wife causes me much trouble. These—like many other roles in my daily repertoire—are roles which I know I play. I may not entirely approve of these parts of myself, but I recognize them; they are familiar, homey. The trouble starts when I use a part of myself I usually bury. I play Tamara, the well-known dance director. I am loud, manipulative, driving, manic. I move constantly. I have to have the others under my spell. I look deeply into each person's eyes. I can't rest. Can't stop. After the scene is over, you are amazed: 'That's really acting. That isn't like you at all.' I, on the other hand, feel slightly nauseated. That's a part of me alright. A part I don't show very often. A part I feel ashamed of. I feel a little shaky lest you now see me as 'that woman.' I need some time to be quiet and get back to being the Eva I know better. Then maybe I can make some sense of what happened. Another therapist helps me understand. I got into a part of my mother which I experienced as very painful as I grew up. A person who frantically covers up her inner turmoil with activity, distraction, and power maneuvers in which others are held in contempt. An isolated, lonely person, certain of her doom."

Role-playing cannot be total make-believe. We can only act ourselves. But, because we are only aware of such a limited part of ourselves at any given time, we often surprise ourselves. The surprise may be a delightful one. We discover a richness of expression which isn't a part of our daily behavior. The discouraged housewife acts the role of her teenage daughter with gusto. For a while, her depression seems to lift. She is no longer slow-moving, soft-voiced, and retiring in her gestures, but becomes mercurial in her emotions, loud, charming, repulsive—a typical teenager. A cantankerous young woman, feared by the other group members for her acid tongue, plays the role of a nurse who relates to an incoming patient with a quiet softness and tenderness. The result is surprise (*I didn't know I had it in me*) and usually delight (*I'm not just depressed, I'm not just sarcastic, and the others in the group can see this other part of me and like it*).

On the other hand, we may surprise ourselves in a way that leaves us feeling confused. After playing Tamara, a woman who had all kinds of qualities I despised, I experienced confusion, a feeling which says in essence: *I don't know what just happened. Playing the role felt very real to me. Yet I feel scared. I didn't know I could act like that. And now that I know, I don't think I can accept it. I don't like that part of me. I can't make any sense of it. I want to forget it. And I want the others to forget it. What if they think that's the real me?* Again, we are looking at the process of bringing into awareness an aspect of our behavior which is not a part of our daily repertory. Confusion, fear, and blocking often result when we meet up with a part of ourselves we don't understand or like. In role-playing, these feelings most often emerge with the playing of negative roles: double-binding, sweetly hostile parents; provocative, teasing wives; withdrawn, icy husbands.

Conflicts of this nature are potentially very productive. If the leader counteracts the participant's tendency to disqualify the experience with phrases such as: "That's not real, anyway. . . . I was only acting . . . in the real situation it would have been different," he can help explore the conflict, and bring into awareness the person's dilemma about showing a part of himself he usually hides. With more understanding, the confusion lifts and the individual makes gains: he may be able to reclaim a part of himself, he may have choices about expressing feelings hitherto repressed. *I learn that I can be strong, active, and vivacious without the desperate restlessness I sensed in my mother. There is a part of me that's like my mother—I'm leading this psychodrama, after all. I also know that I'm very different from her. I can play the role of someone who resembles her without becoming my mother.*

Among groups of people working on psychological problems, there is often a great deal of reluctance to play "negative" roles: the mean mother-in-law, the nagging wife, the stern father. We do not want to appear "bad" in front of others; even if we can justify acting one of the villains as helping another person, we often feel it's bad to show someone that we know just what the villain's game is. One woman in our group had the classical "Jewish mother." Before she could play this part in a scene with a Jewish man, she told us she was afraid of acting the part of her mother—a whining, cajoling, cloying woman very different from the rather quiet daughter. She was afraid playing her mother would be a cruel satire; to her surprise, she learned a great deal about her mother's passionate attachment to her children as she played the role.

Some negative roles carry with them a threat of losing control. Asked to play an angry, punitive father, an individual fears that he would become too angry and actually hit someone during the role-playing. A woman does not want to participate in a scene involving grief for fear that she'll cry. If I suspect these fears, I try to make them explicit so that we can talk about what the next step might be. We may decide that the scene can be stopped whenever the individual feels it necessary. We may provide the son with a pillow so that he can defend himself against Dad, if necessary. We may give Dad a scene in which he does beat a pillow or mattress to help him release some of his anger safely. The woman afraid of her tears may need to do her own grief scene before she can participate in anyone else's. Or she may find out that she has less objection to crying in the group once she's talked about it.

One way in which groups give permission to act out negative roles is, of course, by example. In a new group, I often help give permission by taking on some of these roles myself at first and then, after I have started, I ask if anyone else in the audience is in touch with the person I am playing and could fill in for me. When individuals in a new group do take a chance on portraying negative emotions, I usually make a point of reminding the group that so-and-so did us a favor by taking on this role, and comment that I hope group members realize that the portrayal was quite different from the way he usually presents himself. I make a point of watching to see whether there is any indication of hostility related to the role-playing from other members of the group, so that I can bring it out into the open. If hostility exists unexpressed it will, of course, add to the forces of resistance. After a short time—2 or 3 meetings—a group usually develops an ethos more tolerant of villains. As people play out more negative emotions, they often find it quite rewarding. Everyone knows that being good means giving up all the fun of being bad. In psychodrama groups, individuals can experiment with their "bad" potentialities without getting into trouble for it. In one of my groups, held in a day hospital where there were constant quarrels between the adolescent population and the adult population who shared the same recreation room, some of the most fruitful work came from a role reversal which allowed the adults to run about the stage, turning up the radio and jiving in time to the music, while their teenage counterparts became the moralizing martyrs. In a student group, one of the girls got a great deal of insight into her own life when she played her own mother and saw how helplessly manipulated the others felt by her wiles. Many people spend most of their days in a constricted, inhibited existence which allows for little expression of feeling, positive or negative. What better way to break out than to play someone's swearing, ranting, dissatisfied father?

We timid clinicians are often undone by group resistance. We start developing our own resistances more strongly. We become judges of our own behavior and develop the same doubts and fears we face in our group members: *Should I really try to get them to do something they don't want to do? I don't know how to set up role-playing all that well; can I blame them for saying they don't know how to do it yet? There is something phony about psychodrama. It would be easier just to talk. I've been trained to talk with people. I can do that. Let's just talk and forget the role-playing for now.* If it becomes obvious that someone is having difficulty assimilating a role he's played, or if he is clearly afraid of acting a role which may put him in a negative light, our timidity rises even more. *Do I have the right to ask him to take such a risk? What if it's really bad for him? What if he acts his angry father and he does lose control? Then what do I do? Furthermore, some kinds of strong feelings upset me, too. I don't want him to see me upset. I don't think I want him to take the risk. . . .*

For me, the greatest help has been to know that I can go slowly. I don't have to get the whole group involved in a psychodrama of terrific intensity in a matter of minutes. I can make suggestions and encounter the resistances step by step. I can see my work as giving people choices about whether they want to work or not. There are some people for whom psychodrama does not fit. They've been conscious of doing so much acting all their lives that the very thought of it frightens them. I see myself as giving such individuals as clear a picture as possible of what the next step might be, but I know that I am not responsible for their taking it. If I see myself as supporting group members in making clear, responsible choices, I don't have to view each encounter as a battle in which I'm on one side and the resisting person is on the other. I can see that the resisting person is in conflict: he is here and that says something about his desire to participate, but he's refusing to do so. I know that I can give him support for any clear choice. If he chooses "I won't" for a particular role or for the entire group, I can support that. If he chooses to take the next step, I'll support him there.

For you fellow timid clinicians, I want to repeat that there is no right way to handle a resistance. My hope is that these examples will serve as a basis for developing your own ways of handling the problems that come up in your groups. Personal style is an issue relevant to each and every technique we discuss; it is crucial in attempting to handle the delicate, subtle, important issues of resistances. We all know that children work out many of their questions concerning trust by testing limits; the process remains the same between group members and their leaders. Consider the issues raised in this chapter and experiment with ways of handling them until you feel comfortable. Much of the cohesiveness and trust in the group will depend on your solutions.

Chapter 14

Closure

It is much easier to set up a dramatic situation than to resolve it. The timid clinician often dates his hesitancy concerning psychodramatic techniques to a time when he observed an actual psychodrama. A volunteer from the audience was led through significant scenes in his childhood to a point where he had to make a critical confrontation—with a dead parent, a person whom he wronged, etc. The volunteer confronted the issue with drive and passion. As the scene climaxed, he dissolved into tears. His opponent had nothing more to say. The leader let the audience know that the psychodrama was over. The audience applauded and then filed out of the room. There was a sense of excitement that thrilled many, yet there was also a sense of unfinished business. Many left wondering who would put Humpty-Dumpty back together again.

Confronted by questions about the consequences of such a conclusion, the leader may argue that the catharsis of the drama is healing enough. Further conversation might take away from the dramatic impact and cheat the working individual by diluting an intense experience. *That may be all right for our visiting fireman, the psychodramatist,* the clinician finds himself thinking as he reviews the scene, *but I couldn't do that! I have to keep working with the people I see. I have to pick up the pieces. And he didn't show me anything about how to do that.*

The experience described above has been related to me many times during my work in teaching psychodrama to professionals. *What if I did get the courage to set up a psychodrama, only to find out I didn't know how to end it? Everyone knows there's a warm-up before the psychodrama begins. Is there some way to make the transition from the personal drama of the protagonist back to the group process? Is there a way to end with some feeling of resolution? How can I build trust in the protagonist and the rest of the group members?* These are legitimate questions for the group leader who uses psychodrama as part of his armamentarium.

One problem inherent in the psychodramatic process is that once dramatized, a situation often appears even more powerfully insoluble. The audience identifies with the protagonist, becomes emotionally rooted to his spot and, once the scene is played out, feels as helpless as he does. At the same time, the protagonist is making the transition from an emotionally threatening scene back to the group situation. He often feels vulnerable, somewhat confused, and more than usually in need of support from the group.

In dealing with the problem of closure, I want to avoid two pitfalls. The first can be seen in the scene already described, which often leaves the protagonist without any kind of contact with his audience, without a bridge to the real situation except applause. At best, the protagonist is left strongly in touch with his emotions, and we can hope that this state will lead him to find a way of dealing with the problem he originally presented. At worst, the protagonist feels vulnerable and exploited. He doesn't know what the audience members intend by applauding. Do they find his dilemma entertaining? Do they like him despite his problems? Because of his problems?

The second pitfall is created by our intolerance for the feeling of helplessness which often spreads through an audience that has witnessed a poignantly sad human dilemma. Group members often adopt an artificially self-confident stance. The group process becomes one of intellectualizing. The protagonist in a scene with a rejecting mother is asked a lot of questions: "When did you first feel this way? Did your mother treat the other children the same way? Did your mother ever praise you?" I refer to this maneuver as the group game of "Mr. District Attorney." The protagonist answers—and often finds himself becoming more confused as his intense emotion must be suppressed to enable him to answer the questions put to him by the group. The group members may also intellectualize by suggesting solutions: "Have you tried moving away from home? . . . Why don't you just tell your mother off and walk out? I think you should stop blaming your mother, nobody's perfect. . . . Try just saying nothing when she talks like that, just let her talk." This is the group's version of the game "Psychiatrist," a game which leaves our protagonist feeling that everyone in the group could handle his problem—only *he* apparently found it a dilemma. Both "Mr. District Attorney" and "Psychiatrist" create new problems for the protagonist rather than helping him with the situation in which he finds himself, one on the borderline of public and private.

The first clue for a method of achieving closure may occur within the psychodrama itself. In many situations, *alternative solutions* can be explored psychodramatically. For example, a woman working on an intense conflict concerning her husband and another woman can finish by doing some scenes which take place one year in the future: (1) if she takes a stand and her husband accepts it and stays; (2) if she takes a stand and the husband leaves (acting as if it is ten months since he left); and (3) if she takes no stand and keeps going along with the situation. Or, a young man with conflicts about leaving his mother may profit by setting up a scene during which his fam-

ily discusses his sudden departure and another in which he
talks to his own conscience about his feelings about having
stayed another year. The leader may also explore alternative
solutions by asking the protagonist to repeat a given scene using an alternative approach; i.e., if he has been passive and
quiet in talking with his mother, he could now try an explicit,
verbal approach. Often a feeling of completeness follows the
exploration of alternative solutions. The individual is no
longer viewed as a man trapped in an impossible dilemma: he
has a number of alternatives to weigh and choose from; it is up
to him to find a way that fits. Afterwards, group members can
be encouraged to comment on the part of the scene which
touched them emotionally, and the group can then leave, most
of its business completed.

The situation does not always permit the investigation of alternative solutions. It often happens—because time is short or
because the protagonist is emotionally exhausted—that the exploration of alternative scenes does not fit and group members
experience strong feelings of incompleteness following an intensely emotional scene. At such times, it is important to help
both the protagonist and his fellow group members integrate
the material evoked by the scene. My strategy for accomplish-
ing this goal is to follow the personal psychodramatic work
with group work. In order to avoid the pitfalls of Mr. District
Attorney and Psychiatrist, I structure the discussion highly. I
may use the "collective double" (described more fully in the
chapter, The Double). Briefly, this technique involves saying
something on the order of: "I see that the scene we just did en-
gendered some strong feelings. While we were doing the scene
I noticed some sighs and some tears. How about putting yourself into the scene and speaking as one of the characters. Say
what you might have said, or what you might want to say
now, but first tell us who you are in the scene. For example,
since this was Bob's scene, you might say, 'I'm Bob and I still
feel angry at Mom.' Or, 'I'm Bob's mom and I just don't think
Bob loves me any more.'"

As different group members play out their feelings, the
group tension lessens. The protagonist hears the others speak-

ing directly to his emotions. Group members have an opportunity to put into words those feelings which they experienced
as the protagonist's scene went on.

The question, *"What touched you in what you just saw?"*
is very helpful in eliciting direct personal comment. When I
consult with groups accustomed to intellectual discussion—
discussion groups, study groups, therapy groups with a "talk"
orientation—I usually make it a point to delay the telling
"about" until after there has been some direct response to the
protagonist. I note, "I know you may want to do some talking
about the techniques I used or *about* some other aspects of the
scene you just saw, but right now I don't want you to get away
from your feelings. I know that most of you were very much
involved in what was happening in the scene. Could you say
what touched you?" I usually encourage group members to
make short personal statements directly to the protagonist. We
are already on the road to intellectualization when Mary is allowed to say, "I never knew John was the kind of person who
felt so deeply about his family." We're gossiping *about* John in
his presence. John feels slightly uncomfortable about this, but
can usually find no way to comment. When Mary says to John,
"I was touched by how much feeling you had for your family.
I'd never heard you talk that way before," John gets direct
support and validation of his feelings. From there, it's a small
step to say to Mary, "And how does that scene go in your own
life? Where do those feelings fit in your own family?" in order
to help Mary make a connection between her life and John's.

At such a time, I do not want group members to go into
detail about their own personal situation; I encourage short
statements with the aim of helping each member to make sense
out of his own emotional experience during the hour and giving John validation for his feelings. If I find that someone
wants to go further, I will usually say, "It sounds like you have
something to work on in the same area. Why don't you think
about it, and if it still fits, we could work on it next week." My
general aim in the discussion following psychodramatic work
is to clear the decks, to leave us with as little unfinished business as possible.

Most of the time, the process described above leads to a feeling of closure. While no solutions have been reached, group members have had a chance to express their feelings in relation to the psychodrama and to explore briefly its relevance to their own lives. The group member has made the transition from the feeling "this is John's crisis and it needs an immediate solution," to "this feeling of crisis and frustration occurs in my own life too. Here is an area where I have to do more work. There are a lot of us with similar feelings in this group."

There are times, however, when there is no time for group discussion, or the discussion is not satisfactory. John, for example, may continue to look confused and upset no matter what anyone says, and the other group members feel frustrated and helpless. One or more group members may refuse to abide by the rules I set for the discussion—John is attacked with criticism, suggestions, questions. Or another group member may become so upset as to weep uncontrollably and/or abruptly leave the room. At such a time, I feel that it is very important for the leader to comment on his own feeling of incompleteness. If what's going on can be formulated in words, the group member has the feeling that there's someone in charge who knows what's happening. *The leader can comment that there's a lot of unfinished business.* He can let the group members know that he has expected such meetings to occur, that he doesn't expect each group to leave him with a feeling of satisfaction, and that an incomplete situation doesn't necessarily spell failure. Specifically, the leader may be able to help make some plans for the individual left with the most obviously unresolved feelings. Some of the comments I make at such times are, "We're going to have to stop, and I know that there is a lot of work still to be done. Let's see, John, you look like you're still kind of confused about what happened. Is there someone you can talk with about that before we meet next week?" (If John doesn't have a therapist, some plans may be made that he call another group member or that he come in to see me for a short session mid-week.) Or, "Sometimes, working like this leads us to an impasse and we're all left feeling various degrees of frustration. As much as possible, I'd like you to try to stay with that feeling of frustration. The more you get to know it, even if it is uncomfortable, the more you'll learn about your own impasse." Or, if someone has left abruptly, "I know some of the feeling right now is for Barbara, because she got so upset and left the room. Does anyone want to go after her? Is anyone going to be seeing her? Or do you feel you can trust her to know what's right for her? I would like someone in the group to let her know that we expect her back here next week. Who wants to do it? I can see some of you are still feeling how incomplete this session was in some ways. I'm still feeling some confusion about it also. Let's see what we do with these feelings as the week goes by and report next time." Or, if there is no more time, "We have to stop, and I know there still is a lot more to say and explore. For now, we'll have to leave it the way it is, unfinished. This kind of session is not unusual in a psychodrama and often is very productive. I'll see you next week."

With these comments, the leader gives the message that he continues to be in charge and that he is aware of the negative feelings which have arisen and is prepared to deal with them. Hopefully, the group members will leave feeling a measure of support in a difficult situation.

The timid clinician is often timid in the face of his own expectations. *I should be able to cure the whole group. I should run a group that goes smoothly, especially at the end. If it doesn't, I should keep working until everything is settled.* Here we have it: a gargantuan ego, expecting perfection, looming in the background as the timid clinician hems and haws his way, trying not to make a mistake. My point is, of course, that once our timid clinician rids himself of his own need to master every situation, to bring each conflict to resolution, he will, paradoxically, experience a great deal more self-assurance. Once he can let go of producing the ideal situation, he will be freer to deal with the actual one realistically.

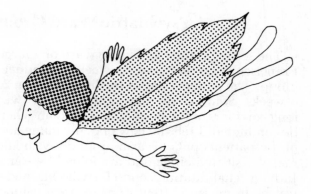

Chapter 15

Psychodramatic Techniques in Use: Two Examples

In the preceding pages, I have tried hard to share with you some ways of going about using specific techniques designed to help structure psychological conflicts in a dramatic way. I want to close this book by relating two examples of my work in some detail. You will recognize the techniques; they no longer need explanation. This section is written with the hope that you will get some feeling for the work as a whole, for my own style and the thoughts and feelings that provide its base, and for the quality of intense absorption and excitement that this work provides for me in its better moments.

A Psychiatric Ward Group

The setting is the psychiatric ward of a large hospital in San Francisco. I go there once a week to conduct a "sociodrama" group. The patients stay at the hospital from 2 or 3 days to 3 or 4 weeks. Some know me; most don't. As we walk down the long corridors of the hospital to the room where the group is to be conducted, I tell the new ones my name and ask theirs. One of the patients puts his arm around my shoulders to welcome me. We sit in a circle and are joined by some staff members: Judy, a rehabilitation counselor who has had some training in psychodrama and attends our sessions regularly; Bob, a resident, verbal, outgoing, and eager to interact with the patients (I sometimes have to rein him in to keep him from going too far into his own problems and away from theirs); and Marie, a student nurse who is so shy she blushes whenever she speaks. I look around the group. Nothing much is happening. People are looking straight ahead or down at the floor. Here goes another meeting. Here goes nothing.

I start to speak. "What I'd like you to do is to think of someone who knows you very well. An important person in your life, like a member of your family, someone you're living with, a close friend. And I'd like you to be that person and describe yourself." Such abstract words to describe such a simple, concrete task. "Your name is Martha and you've got an Aunt Jane; be Aunt Jane telling us about that nuisance Martha who won't get off her duff." The easiest thing would be to demonstrate. Why don't I do it? I don't know. No, I know, but I don't want to go into it.

Someone has understood and is willing to start, a patient, elegantly dressed, black; her name is Valerie. "I'm my friend, Betty Ann. 'Valerie, you're so naive. You just don't know what you're talking about most of the time, and at your age, too!' " I ask her to be Betty Ann and tell us, the group, more about Valerie. "Well, she's just so naive, she'll believe a promise from her boyfriend no matter how many times he's broken it. And she's stubborn! And shy. And very strong, too." I thank her.

We could start to work now, do a scene with Valerie and her boyfriend; but this is the warm-up and I want to hear from the others.

We go around the circle because I sense that it will be easier this way than to ask people to speak when they're ready. Each person gives a response to the task.

Mary Jo is a young woman of Italian background in her twenties. She's been in and out of mental hospitals since she was a child. "I'm my sister Toni. 'Well, Mary Jo is all right but she gets so depressed so easily. I just wish she'd take her pills and get over the depression.' (See, that's all she thinks I have to do, just take my pills.) 'She's alone too much. She ought to get married again and forget about all that mental stuff.' "

Linda, another black woman, about 30, somewhat obese, "I'm my stepmother. She's running down the stairs and then she opens the door and sees me. 'Oh, no, there's that girl again. She just bugs the life out of me always hanging around her father. He doesn't want a girl that age hanging around that much. She just doesn't understand a thing!' "

A disgruntled-looking long-haired man in his late thirties: "Steve is selfish. I'm his wife and I can't get through to him. He's got a lot of problems and that's all he thinks about."

The resident (one rule in my groups is that everyone works, staff included), an intellectual-looking young Jew, "I'm a friend of mine named Polly. 'Bob wants to work all the time. I just don't understand it. Why doesn't he come to Sausalito and enjoy life and sit around a little. Work, work, work.' "

A middle-aged woman in slacks, with untidy hair and a forbidding facial expression: "I can't do it." I repeat the task to her, suggest that maybe she could do it but doesn't want to, get her to talk about her husband a little, but she remains adamant: "I can't do it today." The paradox for the patient: *If I'm sick, I'm helpless. How can they expect me to do something about my problems? How can they expect a helpless person to do anything?*

Jim, a middle-aged, obese, robust-looking man: "I'm my daughter Helen. She's 20. 'Why can't it be like it used to be with my dad? When he worked, we all lived together and we went to the park and on picnics and we had a lot of fun. I want him to get a job so we can get an apartment and live together.' "

There are others, but Jim is the one I pick to start working. He has an urgency in his voice as he talks; he seems to want to say more. Further, I know there are other patients in the room for whom the father–daughter issue is a crucial one. Earlier, when the nurse filled me in on the patients (she spends 10–15 minutes each week giving me a rundown) she told me that Mary Jo's father was dying of Hodgkin's disease, but she hadn't talked about it. We heard Linda talking about her step-mother–father problem earlier.

Jim agrees that he'd like to continue the dialogue with Helen, his daughter. I ask Judy, the rehabilitation counselor, to take her role. Both are requested to move their chairs into the middle of the circle. Judy (in the role of Helen) looks small, crestfallen.

Helen: "When's it going to happen, Dad? You know how great things used to be for us. We did so much together. When are we going to be able to get an apartment?"
Jim: "When I get a job. You know I'm looking every day."
Helen: "Are you really?"
Jim: "Yes, you know I want us to get together as much as you do. I'm confident that it'll all work out shortly."

I ask them to stop the scene for a moment. I'm impressed by how much responsibility Jim says he is taking. He's going to make it all work out right and here he is, in a hospital. He sounds like he's conning, probably furious at his daughter underneath. "Could the two of you tune in to what you're feeling about each other and not saying? Turn to us and tell us some of your secret thoughts."

Jim: "Well, I think she's right. It's time for me to get a job and . . . and work steady again and I want to do what's right for her."

Eva (He's not telling me how he feels. I ask him again.):
"What are you feeling about all that?"

Jim: "Well it would be better if we lived together."

Eva (again I ask): "And how does that make you feel, what's
it like for you to be talking with her?"

Jim: "It makes me feel inadequate. Like a failure."

I thank him and ask Helen to give us her secret thoughts.

Helen: "I really want to live with him, but it's been so long.
I'm getting tired of waiting. He hasn't had a full-time job in
two years. Sometimes I think I shouldn't be waiting for Dad,
that I should be out looking for another husband, to remarry.
Maybe that's what I ought to do. I don't know."

I tell Judy to come and sit in the circle again and I go over to
Jim. "I'd like you to think out loud about this for a minute,
and I'd like to help you by talking with you as part of you, sort
of another voice inside you." He agrees and I begin to double
for him.

Double: "I wish my daughter would really talk like that,
but she never says she wants to be on her own."

Jim: "Yeah, I wish she were more independent. She really
shouldn't be living with me."

Double: "Would I ever tell her that?"

Jim: "No. It would be hard. And I would like it if I could get
a job and we could both live better."

Double: "Am I going to get a job?"

Jim: "Oh, definitely. I'm really looking for one."

Double: "I'm conning now. I don't look that hard."

Jim: "No, I'm not. I don't have the money for the transportation to look every day, but I'd say I look four times a week."

Double: "How long since I had a job?"

Jim: "About ten months."

Double: "Does it really look like it'll change?"

Jim: "Well, not in my line as a draughtsman. I'd probably
just get something temporary again, but I'd have to change my
whole area of job capacity."

Double: "I'm really conning now, always trying to reassure myself and my daughter."
Jim (sighs deeply and looks at me and smiles, shaking his head.)
Double (imitates his gestures.)
Both laugh.

I ask Jim to talk to his daughter Helen one more time, cueing Judy to play the role as Jim describes it—dependent, hopeful that she'll be able to live with Jim. Stammering a little, he tells her that living together might not be so good after all. She's young. "Let's get our own lives straight. Just meet for dinners and stuff, that would be better."

Watching Jim, I feel he's still doing a good bit of conning. Saying what the therapists think is right. It looks as though it's what he wants to say for himself as well, but would he have the courage to say it in the real situation? I doubt it. Two more people stringing each other along on false promises. Anything rather than face one's failings. Anything.

The group members comment. I discourage questions, advice, the ways of pretending that there are simple answers. I ask for feelings. What touched you? What was it like for you? Does Jim's situation strike a chord in you—a similar bind, a similar situation? Mary Jo looks at Jim, "You know, it's hard for kids when their parents suffer. I know when my folks are in trouble I'd do anything to stop it." Her voice is trembling a little, "your daughter probably thinks you can't take care of yourself since you split up with your wife. She wants to help you; be the wife you don't have." For the first time, Jim looks genuinely moved. He nods. It feels right.

I remember that Mary Jo's father is dying of Hodgkin's disease and that Mary Jo has said nothing about this during two hospitalizations within six months. Now I ask Mary Jo about herself as a daughter. The words burst out of her, "I think about it all the time. If one of them dies, I'm the one that has to take care of them. They're old and helpless. I couldn't leave them alone. My brother wouldn't do it. He never did give a damn. And my sister has her own family to take care of. I think and think about what it would be like growing old as a spinster, taking care of my dad, but I never get anywhere." She is pretty and young, and still I could see her going through with it. I ask her if she would like to do more work in this area by thinking out loud some more, with Judy as a double. I consider setting up a scene with her parents, but choose the doubling because I want Mary Jo to confront herself, to get in touch with her own conflicting feelings. She agrees.

Mary Jo: "I don't even see them or talk to them that much but they're so good to me. My father sends me money. I don't even want him to but he still does and my mom really cares about how I'm doing."

Double: "I really feel I owe them something."

Mary Jo: "It's true. They've had such a hard life. My father's just this simple Italian and he worked like a dog all his life and then they bought this house just last year. After all the worries with us—one of the kids died real early—this was finally going to be the reward. They moved into this little beach house where they are now and he's sick and she's getting weaker. *(Her whole body is beginning to tremble.)* My dad can't do anything for himself. He can't even boil an egg."

Double: "I have to help. Somebody has to. I'll do it. I owe it to them."

Mary Jo: "I do. It was so hard for them all the time and I've been going to hospitals with this trouble all my life. I do owe him a lot. And when I picture one of them helpless and see the lumps growing in my dad's throat. . . ." *(She's crying. It sounds as though she hasn't cried in a long time; a high, screeching wail.)*

Linda gets up out of her chair and starts to walk across the room. "I just can't stand to see anyone crying." Mary Jo gets up. "I'll stop. I don't want to upset anybody." Marian, the nurse, quietly talks to Linda and persuades her to stay, while I urge Mary Jo to continue. She does.

Double: "I can't bear to think of how helpless they are because I feel so helpless myself so often."

Mary Jo: "I think I'm the only one that knows what it's like. But I really am. The others won't do anything and they won't listen to me if I try to talk about it. I'm the crazy one. I'm crazy. My sister even said it to me."

Double: "So I'm ready to give up my own life."

Mary Jo (sighs deeply): "I can't get out of it. I'm not getting married again anyway. I don't have any kids."

Double: "I'm not worth anything. At least I love my parents."

Mary Jo: "I do and they look so old and frail *(starts to cry again)*. They're in their seventies and they're going to be dead." *(Cries.)*

Double (waiting, letting Mary Jo's tears subside): "Why don't I count? There must be some way to be a good daughter and still live my own life."

Mary Jo: "It's true. I know that's right but I just don't know how to do it."

Mary Jo looks at me. "I want to stop now." I nod my head, "Yes." Mary Jo looks softer. She has stopped trembling. There is a quiet feeling in the room. Everyone in touch with his own pain. I ask the group members to relate what they're experiencing. Various people express empathy. I know they mean it. We were feeling with Mary Jo. And ourselves. Valerie says she was ready to do the same thing, just go back to Texas and take care of her folks.

Bob, the resident, reminds Mary Jo of her willingness to stop working because Linda was upset. "You count everyone else first."

I ask Mary Jo whether she has brought up this problem with her own therapist. She replies that she's talked about it but it's been hard to get really close to what's bothering her, like today. She wants to work on it more in therapy. She's going to ask her therapist to meet with her four times a week instead of three.

Valerie looks at Bob and Mary Jo. "You know, I've learned something today. I'm the same way. I always put everyone else first. I expect to be bothered and upset, but I don't think I ever have the right to bother anybody. Wow. I really learned something today."

I nod my head. I feel good about the work. It's a good beginning for Mary Jo.

"See you next week." The group is over.

A Couples' Group

This is a couples' group which meets once a week for three hours. The six couples know each other well. They're here to work on marital problems and they have developed an ethos which usually enables them to work hard and intensely. Many have made changes for the better. They've spurred each other on. My co-therapist and I use many experiential techniques in the group: role-playing, Gestalt dialogues, sensory awareness, and a television-feedback system run by a cameraman who has become a third therapist. Often, the work centers on individual growth. After the initial period during which a couple either clears away the destructive marital games or leaves the group, there is usually a time where each works on his own life goals.

Herbert is starting to tell us about his decision to take a leave of absence from a Ph.D. program in psychology. After promising a program of challenging experimentation with new techniques, the course turned out to be dull and conservative. Other group members express surprise. Herb is a lawyer who had impressed many of them by his plan to change careers. Now what? The session turns to a peculiar kind of superficial question-and-answer game which I later label as a vocational counseling session. "How long is the leave of absence? Do you think you'll really go back? If you can't get your Ph.D. will you continue to practice law? Aren't you afraid to just drop it? You were so happy that you got into the program."

I'm not happy with what's going on. No feelings are coming out. Just a lot of talk. But they know that as well as I do. I try to tell myself that I don't have to make anything happen, just wait until something does. But it's hard on me when they don't work. Herb comes through.

"I'm not getting anywhere. It's just like talking to my father: 'You need a career, Herb.' I used to think he was right but just don't anymore!"

Herb's wife tells him that she thinks he's been closer to people since he's worked less.

Herb agrees. "I sure talk a lot to my parents about it though. They think everything's going to be lost if I'm not a something. They really panicked when I left the firm."

I feel relieved. Herb is getting into a real conflict within himself: a something versus a nothing. No wonder he's stuck. Maybe we can do some Gestalt work.

Eva: "All that small talk is beginning to make sense to me, Herb. And the fact that you took a leave of absence instead of quitting. It's as though you're suspended, not making a decision, not coming to terms with yourself in some way, and we've been suspended with you."

Herb: "It's that I really think I'm just going to totally drop out and then maybe I'll be happy. I don't know."

Eva: "How about a dialogue between Herb now and Herb the dropout. *(He is sitting on a pillow against the wall; I throw him another large pillow.)* Put the dropout Herb on the pillow there in front of you. Write a script between you and him."

Herb: "Wow . . . *(smiling and shaking his head)* you're really important to me. You're strong. I feel stuck here."

Eva: "Change pillows and get his reaction." *(He does.)*

Dropout: "You're scared, but you know better. You know you don't really need all that crap. Quit the games. Just be."

Herb: "Yeah, but you just tell me what not to do. So I quit the games? What then?"

Dropout: "Wow . . . *(Herb turns to the group)*. I'm really feeling scared. Really scared now."

Eva: "How are you experiencing being scared?"

Herb: "I can't seem to breathe very well. . . . And I feel shaky. I thought this was more than just a job crisis."

He really looks scared. I can feel it. So can other members of the group. Some are shifting in their seats. I feel excited, I don't know just where we're going but I know it's important. I hope I can handle it. The important thing is not to lead him. To take him wherever he's going. Be in charge without being in control. It's hard when he looks so scared.

Eva: "Where in your body do you experience the shaking?"

Herb: "It's not really shaking. Trembling. My upper body. My shoulders. My arms. *(Herb tunes into himself now. It is obvious he no longer notices the other group members.)* I'm really scared."

Eva: "Shut your eyes and see if you can go into your fear. Give yourself a fantasy of what it's like. A landscape. An atmosphere."

Herb: "It's like floating. Like a leaf in the wind."

Eva: "Be the leaf. Tell us about your existence. Where you are. What you look like."

Herb: "I'm green and healthy and the wind is blowing me around. I'm floating all over the place and I'm being carried. *(Smiles.)* I like it. Just floating around. Nope. I'm afraid."

Eva: "What are you afraid of?"

Herb: "I'm afraid I'm going to drop. I don't want to. I really don't want to drop." *(Smiling. He looks like he knows what he's saying—the metaphor of suspension is still being carried out.)*

Eva: "So drop." *(I'm smiling too, but I know I'm asking him to do something which isn't easy.)*

Herb: "*I really* don't want to. *(Still smiling.)* O.K. Suddenly the wind stops carrying me. I drop to the ground." *(His face changes. He looks serious.)*

Eva: "What's it like there?"

Herb: "I'm on the ground and I don't like it. I want to be back on the tree. I want to hold on." *(His voice is trembling.)*

Eva: "What's it like now? What do you look like?"

Herb: "Brown. Shriveled up. *(He is trembling slightly.)* I don't want to go any further." *(Looking up at me.)*

This is it. What Fritz Perls called the death layer. Herb is really in it. I wonder if the others are thinking the same thing I am: he looks so shaken and so far away. How will he come out of this? No one makes any attempt to break the atmosphere, to rescue Herb. My co-therapist looks at Herb.

Co-therapist: "You haven't finished yet. You still have further to go."
Herb: "Where?"
Co-therapist: "Into the earth."
Herb: "I know, but I'm not ready."
Eva: "What are you feeling now?"
Herb: "Cold. And very, very lonely."
Eva: "What happened to the trembling?"
Herb: "It's gone. I feel quiet now. A stillness inside me. Very quiet and still."

I look around the group. Those words have a lot of meaning to each of us. Alone. Quiet. Still. They're hard to face, those words. I want to help Herb work through this without invading his loneliness. I still don't know how he'll come back to us.

Eva: "Talk to your stillness."
Herb: "I know you but I'm not ready for you."
Stillness: "I'm very large. I'm here. I'm waiting for you."
Herb: "I know, but I'm not ready. I still have a lot of things I want to do."

Herb is not looking at anyone. He is still quite alone. I ask him whether he can come back to the group, to take a look at us. He obliges, but I see that he isn't making any real contact yet. I have been noticing his wife every now and then during the work; she has looked very involved. Now she is sitting by; her eyes are full of feeling for Herb. I ask Herb to take a look at Anne. What follows is a rare moment of understanding. An intimate moment. He really sees her. She looks at him, holds his hands, sees him withdraw slightly and lets him know in words that she has understood his struggle and felt some of it herself.

Realizing that I'm alone and that you're alone too: the words all marital games are designed to conceal. And the paradox. When the experience is permitted, togetherness is possible. Herb and Anne are hugging. There isn't a dry eye in the house. I feel a combination of relief and estrangement. The work is completed, but I've had to hold back my own feelings. I ask the other group members what the experience was like for them. Most of them express being deeply touched—by the experience of their own loneliness, Herb's and Anne's togetherness, the realization that the human condition is experienced so similarly by all of us. One guy says he lost track of what was going on early in the work and followed his own thoughts. That's O.K. also. The group's comments allow me to get back to my own feelings again. I'm in touch with how moved I feel; there are tears in my eyes. There's a welcome sense of completion. The work has been good.

Epilogue

When I was developing the techniques in this book, the climate of psychotherapy was different from what it is now; it was dominated by a psychoanalytic point of view. Therapy was commonly regarded as a process occurring between two people: a doctor and a patient. The main ingredient of the process was talk about the patient's life. Only a few clinicians, clearly outside the mainstream, practiced anything different, such as group therapy and psychodrama.

In the late '50s and early '60s came the challengers, the change-makers. From psychiatry, social work, sociology, psychology—disciplines that had been infused with knowledge from psychoanalysis and had much of their own to contribute—came individuals who explored new ways of doing psychotherapy. Times and symptoms were changing. More and more people were interested in receiving psychotherapy. Instead of seeking help for seriously impairing psychological symptoms such as hysterical paralysis, they often sought more elusive qualities such as "more effective functioning," or simply "growth." The psychotherapy group came into prominent use. The one-to-one, exclusively verbal approach to psychotherapy began to recede from the dominant position it had held for so many years.

Fritz Perls, Virginia Satir, Don Jackson, Jay Haley, and Stanley Kellerman, to name a few, developed innovative techniques that highlighted immediate experiencing. Joint interviewing of couples and families, anathema in conservative

165

psychiatry, was pioneered by John Bell, by Viriginia Satir, and by a few others. Earlier, Moreno in New York had developed psychodrama as a therapeutic tool and now his influence grew, and other therapists, I among them, developed their own methods. There seemed to be a wave of change washing over what had become an arid landscape. The revival of psychodrama was part of that fresh wave.

As a consequence of the focus on experience, the scope of therapy broadened. Other disciplines helpful in expanding awareness and consciousness came into use as adjuncts to psychotherapy. Drama, dance, art, yoga, zen practice, mime, aikido, massage, video-feedback, and so on, all became a part of the therapeutic armamentarium. The wave took on larger proportions. On it rode many therapists—now called group facilitators, leaders, or counselors—whose training in the specific new discipline was usually excellent but whose clinical skills were frequently limited to little more than enthusiasm and good will. I viewed their arrival with mixed feelings. They were young and enthusiastic, and brought new skills that enlivened and challenged the old regime. But could they do the job? Did they have any idea of the complexities of human relationships?

The early challengers (myself included) had respected the establishment they were challenging. They were well-trained, conscientious, frequently highly credentialed clinicians. What they did not foresee was that expanding therapeutic techniques and making them widely available could have a detrimental result: namely, that the highly valued discipline and knowledge of clinical skills which they possessed could no longer be taken for granted in other therapists.

What do I mean by clinical skills? I am referring to the skills that let us assess what is wrong and find a way to help it become less so. Clinical skills provide the basis for doing our work. In any clinical situation, they include sensitivity to the moment, a long-range understanding of what is normal and what is possible, and the ability to communicate at the right time in an effective way. The skilled clinician knows his own potential and can turn away the patient whom he feels ill-equipped to treat. These skills cannot be developed quickly. They require years of devoted, intensive study of human beings, their patterns of growth, their inner processes, and their interrelationships—study in a training program with the guidance and supervision of an experienced clinician.

When I began to write this book, I wanted primarily to encourage those timid clinicians—members of the old school—who were eager to try some of the newer techniques but too shy to do so. They knew a great deal, were often already successful in their practice when they came to me as students, and felt that the experiential techniques would help them work in a more powerful, richer way. I wanted (and still want) to help them overcome their timidity when confronted by new forms, to teach them that it is all right to role-play, to move chairs and desks, to explore in an active, spontaneous manner.

The more recent change in psychotherapy has oriented me to another goal. I want to help the talented newcomers develop their clinical skills. Many of these new students have no fear of active techniques. Typical is the student who, during his first interview with a family, has them reverse roles, divide up into teams, each commenting on the other's behavior, and do breathing and relaxation exercises. His cup may run over with techniques, yet he experiences difficulties. Without academic discipline behind him, and lacking years of first-hand experience, he seems unable to understand what is happening in the contexts he so actively creates. He feels like a recreational counselor: he can set up activities and enliven the interview, but he lacks the skills with which he could help the family integrate the activities so that they can change. He has a feeling neither of continuity during his hour nor of closure at the end of it.

It is my hope that this book offers some help in developing clinical skills. The discussion of such concepts as doubling, closure, and resistances is intended to help a student integrate his techniques clinically, so that the experiences he arranges for his patients can do what they are supposed to do—lead to individual growth. In the last ten years, psychodrama has become a more and more familiar technique. It lends a richer, more exciting, and immediate experience to many of the issues facing the patient, the therapist, and any others involved in his treatment. My hope is that this book will continue to further its use.

— Eva Leveton

San Francisco
June, 1976

Glossary

Many of the terms that follow are already familiar to the reader. I have not tried to define them in the conventional sense. A dictionary can be consulted for that purpose. Instead, I've tried to provide the reader with definitions and short explanations of words used in a peculiar way by psychodramatists, experiential therapists, and theater folk. I've also tried to give the reader a very quick introduction to some of the individuals whose original work enhanced the progress of my eclecticism.

acting: A specific discipline, the accomplishment of which lets the actor take part in theater or film work. Acting is often confused with role-playing, which is, in fact, only a small part of the discipline comprising mime, voice production, body movement and character-building, and many other techniques.

archetype: Here used in the sense that Karl Jung used it, as prototype for oft-repeated personalities: the wise old man, the helpless maiden, the young hero, the earth-mother, for example.

ben Ali, Bobker: Practicing psychodramatist in Pasadena, California, who was trained by J. L. Moreno.

Berne, Eric: Author of the books *Transactional Analysis in Psychotherapy* and *Games People Play*; founder of transactional analysis, a system of individual and group dynamics using group therapy and "games analysis" as major treatment modes.

bridge: Used to describe the connection the leader makes between the various scenes in a psychodrama and the commentary that precedes and follows them.

catharsis: The discharge of intense emotion through its expression in a psychodrama, as, for example, the expression of hitherto unexpressed grief or anger in a particular scene.

childhood recall: The vivid and detailed recall of childhood experiences not readily available to the individual.

conflicts: The collisions of opposing forces that are the heart of psychodrama. Whether the struggle is inter- or intrapersonal, both sides in the conflict provide the dialogue essential to psychodrama.

control: Here used in the sense of an individual's ability to remain in charge of his emotions. The leader must be aware that psychodrama may challenge this control and cause unpredicted outbursts of tears or anger.

director: The person in charge of a specific psychodrama. (There may be several directors in a group where each psychodrama has a different director.)

distancing: Here used to mean (1) putting the other person off, at a psychological distance, or (2) locating the other person in the physical distance that fits the perceived psychological relationship.

double: The representation by a person of an unexpressed part of another's existence, otherwise called alter ego or, sometimes, shadow.

encounter: A psychotherapeutic approach centering on a dialogue between peers where each is expected to comment frankly and honestly on the other's behavior.

Esalen: A spa with hot springs in Big Sur, California, used as a center for learning. Both Fritz Perls and Virginia Satir were long-term resident teachers there.

experiential: Here used to describe a therapeutic technique that actively provides the individual with a new life experience, as contrasted to the more analytic "talking" therapies.

fantasy: All role-playing requires fantasy, but here we use the word to refer to material outside the real life situation of the role-player. A fantasy role is imagined in the sense that it takes place in another country, another life zone, or dreams; a person can change into an animal, a rock, a much richer or poorer individual, etc.

Gestalt: Here used to refer to a system of psychiatric dynamics developed by Fritz Perls. In this context, Gestalt, the German word for figure, refers to the individual's need to complete his psychologically unfinished business, lest he spend his life repeating the same patterns, just as the hungry person spends his time with recurrent fantasies of food until his hunger is satisfied.

Haley, Jay: Member of the original Mental Research Institute Group that developed systems and communications theory and the concept of the double bind. Presently director of the Family Therapy Institute in Washington, D.C., and author of *Uncommon Therapy* and *Problem-Solving Therapy*.

intellectualization: A psychological defense mechanism in which a threat is deprived of its emotional content through overuse of intellectual analysis; a frequent defense in psychodrama groups, especially during the discussion period.

Jackson, Don: Member of the original M.R.I. Group (see Jay Haley). Editor of *Human Communication*, volumes 1 and 2, a compendium of this group's work.

Keleman, Stan: Teacher of Bio-Energetics (a system combining body awareness and psychological dynamics), therapist, and author of *Living your Dying*.

Korn, Richard: Practicing psychodramatist in Berkeley, California, and one of the directors of the Berkeley Institute for Training in Psychodrama; trained by J. L. Moreno.

leader: Person in charge of the entire psychodrama group, which can have several directors of separate scenes but only one leader.

Lewin, Kurt: Founder of Field Theory, a system of social psychology that stresses the necessity of considering context in the analysis of any situation.

magic shop: Psychodramatic technique that uses the device of a shop dealing in human qualities to examine them.

model: To demonstrate how to play a role, comment, or behave spontaneously; an important aspect of psychodramatic leadership.

Moreno, J. L.: Founder of psychodrama as a system of psychiatric dynamics and a technique of teaching and psychotherapy. Author of *Psychodrama*, volumes 1, 2, and 3.

patient: A person under sufficient stress to pay for the services of another to help reduce it.

Perls, Fritz: Founder of Gestalt Therapy. Author of *Ego, Hunger and Aggression; Gestalt Therapy* (co-authors: Ralph Hefferline and Paul Goodman); *Gestalt Therapy Verbatim; The Gestalt Approach: Eyewitness to Therapy;* and *In and Out of the Garbage Pail*.

portrayal: Here used to describe the attempt of one person to role-play specific aspects of another person's personality.

process: The manner of doing something. Here we refer to the process of psychodrama or to the process of its leader in order to describe, for example, *how* the psychodrama works or *how* the leader makes decisions.

protagonist: The main character in a psychodrama.

psychodrama: Term originated by Moreno, which we use in a more general sense than he does, to designate any role-playing in the service of personal growth or investigation.

resistance: A psychological defense designed to protect the individual from the dangers of change.

resolution: The psychodrama achieves resolution when there is a lessening of tension accompanied by a different point of view, a new solution, or insight.

risk: Used when a person takes a leap into the psychological unknown.

role-playing: Taking part in a psychodrama. It is important not to confuse role-playing with acting. Role-playing is a spontaneous activity depending solely on the participant's ability to fit himself into the role assigned to him through his reactions to the others in the scene. Acting, on the other hand, begins with role-playing but involves a complex discipline requiring the individual to be able to learn scripts, play in a way suitable for stage or film, and repeat performances in exact detail as often as required.

role-reversal: When two role-playing individuals take each other's roles. (In a father-son dialogue, for example, the father plays the son's part while the son plays the father.)

Satir, Virginia: Author of *Conjoint Family Therapy* and *People Making*. A leader in the development of family therapy and the evolution of experiential techniques.

satire: Here used to highlight the use of irony and humorous contrast in a psychodrama to help an individual see his problems from a new perspective.

scene: A part of a psychodrama with a beginning, an end, and no change in characters. Leaders often find it useful to divide a psychodrama into various scenes, each with a specific purpose.

sculpture: An experiential technique requiring an individual to shape another person (or persons) into the posture he feels appropriately describes an emotional relationship.

sensory awareness: A therapeutic technique designed to provide the individual with greater information about his body and his five senses.

sociodrama: Moreno's term designating dramatic material relevant to social issues facing the whole group, for example, racial conflicts in a group with both Caucasian and black members.

sociogram: A psychodramatic technique requiring the individual to make a living picture of a group of persons important to him by placing them at the physical distance appropriate for their psychological relationship.

stage: Here used to designate any area where a psychodrama takes place.

Stanislavsky, Konstantin: Founder of a school of acting based on a recapturing of the personal experience of the actor or "sense-memory," from which "method acting" is derived. Many of his exercises are relevant to psychodramatic work. Author of *An Actor Prepares* and *My Life in Art*.

strategy: A plan developed by a psychodrama leader or director for a specific purpose in a particular psychodrama.

style: The manner of doing one's work; that which is personal and idiosyncratic in the psychodrama leader's performance.

timid: Easily frightened, wanting boldness or courage.

warm-up: The initial activity in a psychodrama group; designed to encourage maximum participation and spontaneity as well as to provide group members and leader with material for further work.

work: Everything relating to the development of psychodrama; "work" may well be "play" if it relates to psychodrama but not if it relates to such defenses against it as chit-chat and intellectualization.